COPING WITH INFANT OR FETAL LOSS

The Couple's Healing Process

Brunner/Mazel Psychosocial Stress Series
Charles R. Figley, Ph.D., Series Editor

1. *Stress Disorders among Vietnam Veterans*, Edited by Charles R. Figley, Ph.D.
2. *Stress and the Family Vol. 1: Coping with Normative Transitions*, Edited by Hamilton I. McCubbin, Ph.D., and Charles R. Figley, Ph.D.
3. *Stress and the Family Vol. 2: Coping with Catastrophe*, Edited by Charles R. Figley, Ph.D. and Hamilton I. McCubbin, Ph.D.
4. *Trauma and Its Wake: The Study and Treatment of Post-Traumatic Stress Disorder*, Edited by Charles R. Figley, Ph.D.
5. *Post-Traumatic Stress Disorder and the War Veteran Patient*, Edited by William E. Kelly, M.D.
6. *The Crime Victim's Book, Second Edition*, by Morton Bard, Ph.D. and Dawn Sangrey.
7. *Stress and Coping in Time of War: Generalizations from the Israeli Experience*, Edited by Norman A. Milgram, Ph.D.
8. *Trauma and Its Wake Vol. 2: Traumatic Stress Theory, Research, and Intervention*, Edited by Charles R. Figley, Ph.D.
9. *Stress and Addiction*, Edited by Edward Gottheil, M.D., Ph.D., Keith A. Druley, Ph.D., Steven Pashko, Ph.D., and Stephen P. Weinstein, Ph.D.
10. *Vietnam: A Casebook*, by Jacob D. Lindy, M.D., in collboration with Bonnie L. Green, Ph.D., Mary C. Grace, M.Ed., M.S., John A. MacLeod, M.D., and Louis Spitz, M.D.
11. *Post-Trumatic Therapy and Victims of Violence*, Edited by Frank M. Ochberg, M.D.
12. *Mental Health Response to Mass Emergencies: Theory and Practice*, Edited by Mary Lystad, Ph.D.
13. *Treating Stress in Families*, Edited by Charles R. Figley, Ph.D.
14. *Trauma, Transformation, and Healing: An Integrative Approach to Theory, Research, and Post-Traumatic Therapy*, by John P. Wilson, Ph.D.
15. *Systemic Treatment of Incest: A Therapeutic Handbook*, by Terry Trepper, Ph.D. and Mary Jo Barret, M.S.W.
16. *The Crisis of Competence: Transitional Stress and the Displaced Worker*, Edited by Carl A. Maida, Ph.D., Norma S. Gordon, M.A., and Norman L. Farberow, Ph.D.
17. *Stress Management: An Integrated Approach to Therapy*, by Dorothy H. G. Cotton, Ph.D.
18. *Trauma and the Vietnam War Generation: Report of the Findings from the National Vietnam Veterans Readjustment Study*, by Richard A. Kulka, Ph.D., William E. Schlenger, Ph.D., John A. Fairbank, Ph.D., Richard L. Hough, Ph.D., B. Kathleen Jordan, Ph.D., Charles R. Marmar, M.D., Daniel S. Weiss, Ph.D., and David A. Grady, Psy.D.
19. *Strangers at Home: Vietnam Veterans Since the War*, Edited by Charles R. Figley, Ph.D. and Seymour Leventman, Ph.D.
20. *The National Vietnam Veterans Readjustment Study: Tables of Findings and Technical Appendices*, by Richard A. Kulka, Ph.D., William E. Schlenger, Ph.D., John A. Fairbank, Ph.D., Richard L. Hough, Ph.D., B. Kathleen Jordan, Ph.D., Charles R. Marmar, M.D., Daniel S. Weiss, Ph.D.
21. *Psychological Trauma and The Adult Survivor: Theory, Therapy, and Transformation*, by I. Lisa McCann, Ph.D., and Laurie Anne Pearlman, Ph.D.
22. *Coping with Infant or Fetal Loss: The Couple's Healing Process*, by Kathleen R. Gilbert Ph.D., and Laura S. Smart, Ph.D.

BRUNNER/MAZEL PSYCHOSOCIAL STRESS SERIES NO. 22

COPING WITH INFANT OR FETAL LOSS

The Couple's Healing Process

Kathleen R. Gilbert, Ph.D.
Laura S. Smart, Ph.D.

BRUNNER/MAZEL Publishers • NEW YORK

Library of Congress Cataloging-in Publication Data
Gilbert, Kathleen R.
      Coping with infant or fetal loss : the couple's healing process /
Kathleen R. Gilbert, Laura S. Smart
         p.   cm.—(Brunner/Mazel psychosocial stress series : no. 22)
      Includes bibliographical references and index.
      ISBN 0-87630-679-2
      1. Perinatal death—Psychological aspects.   2. Infants—Death—
Psychological aspects.   3. Bereavement—Psychological aspects.
4. Grief therapy.   5. Marital psychotherapy.   6. Parent and Child.
I. Smart, Laura S.   II. Title.   III. Series.
      [DNLM: 1. adaptation, Psychological.   2. Death—in infancy &
childhood.   3. Fetal Death.   4. Grief.   5. Parents—psychology.
   6. Social Support.   W1 BR917TB no.22 / BF 789.D4 G465c]
   RG631.G56   1992
155.9'37—dc20
   DNLM/DLC
for Library of Congress   92-16166
                                                                            CIP

Published by
BRUNNER/MAZEL, INC.
19 Union Square West
New York, New York 10003

Manufactured in the United States of America

10 9 8 7 6 5 4 3 2 1

Contents

Preface

Some years ago, a friend said to one of the authors, "We are not victims; we are survivors!" In that moment, the listener was not sure that she was a survivor. But over time, she became one.

This series examines the experience of survivors of traumatic events, the often slow and painful process of becoming a survivor. This book examines the healing process of 27 married couples who experienced miscarriage, stillbirth, or the death of their infant; that is, their movement toward becoming survivors, as individuals and as couples. We listened to them as they told us about the time of their loss and what followed: how they helped each other, and sometimes how they did not help each other; how their physicians, nurses, family members, friends and co-workers responded to their loss; what they learned in the process.

Kathleen Gilbert wrote the first drafts of chapters 2, 3, 4, and 5 and Appendix A. Laura Smart wrote the first draft of chapters 1, 6, 7, and 8.

This book is the story of 54 parents, who shared their experiences with us. We thank them for their generosity. We feel that it is a privilege to have heard firsthand such intimate stories. Although each loss experience is unique, these experiences also fit into a larger framework of the healing process. The experiences of our respondents are, in this book, woven into a larger tapestry that provides a framework for understanding the loss experiences of individuals and couples.

Although this book is intended primarily for professionals working with bereaved parents who have experienced pregnancy loss and infant death, it will also be of interest to many bereaved parents. The book tells the story of how members of intact couples—marital survivors as well as survivors of bereavement—dealt with their loss, each other, and others who tried to help them. The path of healing was not smooth or direct. There were cul-de-sacs and false turns for most of these survivors.

We wish to thank the many people who made this book possible. Our series editor, Charles Figley, a friend and mentor, provided encouragement at all stages of this project. The interviewing process was made easier by our capable co-interviewers, Rebecca Adams and Holly Carlfeldt. Our thanks also go out to Britton Wood for his ability to take our ideas and show how they can be applied in therapy.

In the course of writing this book, we found support and encouragement from our colleagues. We would like to acknowledge the helpful comments and suggestions we received from Judith Lasker, Peggy Quinn, and Joseph Baumgart, M.D.

Each of us holds a debt of gratitude for support and encouragement received from our own university communities: Kathleen, to her colleagues at Indiana University and especially, her Department Chair, John Seffrin; and Laura to Northern Illinois University, which provided financial support for her during her sabbatical leave, as well as to her colleagues and her Department Chair, Earl Goodman.

We would like to thank our publisher, Brunner/Mazel, Inc., and in particular, our editors Natalie Gilman and Suzi Tucker.

We would like to thank our families for their love and support throughout the process of writing this book. Thanks to our husbands, Steven Gilbert and Roger Cohn, and our daughters, Kimberly and Rebecca Gilbert and Caitlin Cohn. The parts of this book that Laura wrote are dedicated to the memory of her son, Daniel Russell Cohn, whose death remains a mystery.

1

Introduction and Overview

In the labor rooms, those people have a lot of training and they have a lot of experience [but] they don't know how to communicate that to the parents. [The nurses and doctors] may have the same feelings of loss that you have. And they may feel they'd be better off not talking. [But] they need to bring up some of the issues. . . . The nurses need to be trained to ask the parents if they have some questions. They didn't say [to us], "Do you have any questions about this? Do you understand?" [Matt]*

INTRODUCTION

Pregnancy loss and infant death take place within a cultural context. A generation ago, stillborn babies were whisked away from the parents, in the belief that not seeing the baby helped in the recovery process. (Indeed, even some of our respondents were not shown their infants.) Some of the parents of our respondents had experienced deaths of their own infants, and our respondents commented that they were surprised that the grandparents were not more helpful to the second generation. Today, there is heightened sensitivity to fetal and infant death, perhaps in part because of elective abortion issues. However, the old ways of dealing with fetal and infant death (ignoring

---

*In order to protect the confidentiality of participants, pseudonyms were used. To assist the reader, a list of pseudonyms organized by couples is included as Appendix D.

and denying the loss) coexist with newer ways, which include naming the baby, taking pictures of him or her, keeping mementoes, and talking about the baby.

Until quite recently, sources of support for bereaved parents were private and idiosyncratic. Conventional wisdom was that it was best to forget the incident and get on with life. In the 1980s, there was more interest in the topic, although much of the research focused on the mother's reaction. In this book, we present qualitative data from 27 married couples. Our view is that pregnancy loss and infant death affect not only mothers and fathers, but the marriage as well. Because our respondents told us that medical personnel are crucial providers of information and support, our primary audience is family care nurses and physicians. Because they so often serve families immediately and long after such a loss, a secondary audience is family therapists. Finally, because we are both family scientists, another secondary audience is family scientists with an interest in family stress.

In qualitative research, it is appropriate to provide the baseline of inquiry; that is, to inform the reader how the topic of study was chosen. One of the authors had a close friend who had experienced a premature birth that resulted in the death of the infant. Shortly after this unfortunate occurrence, the other author experienced the fetal death of her first child. From these deaths came the desire to learn more about the recovery process of bereaved couples. The methodology that we employed is explained more fully in Appendix A. Here, we will give a brief overview of the methodology.

OVERVIEW OF METHODOLOGY

Twenty-seven married couples who had experienced a fetal or an infant death were interviewed using a semistructured format. All of the spouses were members of intact couples who had been married at the time of the fetal or infant death and who had remained married until the time of data collection. All couples, except one interviewed at their place of business, were interviewed in their homes. Partners were interviewed simultaneously and separately by the authors and two research assistants.

In addition to selected demographic data, the interview, following a general interview guide (Patton, 1980), sought behavioral and subjective aspects of the parents' experience. Four content areas were covered by the interviews: First, they were asked about their experiences immediately following the death of their child, including what needed to be done, what they needed from their spouse, and what they and their spouse did for each other. Second, they were asked about recurrent grief. Third, changes in themselves and their marriage were examined. Finally, they were asked to make recommendations to professionals, family members, friends, and other bereaved parents.

Data Analysis

Data generated by the interviews were analyzed qualitatively (Lincoln & Guba, 1985; Patton, 1980), using abstract categorization and discussion of the meaning, application, and implications of the data (Lofland & Lofland, 1984). The data were analyzed inductively. The interpretation of the data was ideographic; that is, the emphasis was on particularization rather than generalization (Lincoln & Guba, 1985).

OVERVIEW OF THE BOOK

The purpose of this book is to explore the dynamics of husband–wife interaction during the recovery from parental bereavement following pregnancy loss and infant death. Previous writers on pregnancy loss and infant death have focused upon the mother. Our research supports the idea that *in general* mothers are more affected by this loss than are fathers, but we note that there are exceptional cases. Helping professionals should not assume that in any given case the mother is more deeply affected than the father. Furthermore, the death of a child impacts not just married individuals, but the marital system. Our goal is to illuminate this process.

In Chapter 2, we provide an overview of theories of grief and traumatic stress. First, we briefly describe stage theories of grief, with a focus on the Parkes/Bowlby model. We then describe stage theories of family adaptation. Then, following a brief critique of the stage theory model, process theory models are examined. Specifically, we state that the "resolution" of grief involves forming a healing theory through the reworking of parental assumptions about how the world works. For the reconstruction of meaning, we note the importance of social support, particularly within the couple relationship. These themes (the reworking of assumptions to form a healing theory and the importance of social support within and outside the marital relationship) are threads that run throughout the book.

The focus in Chapter 3 is upon the grieving process at the individual level. The death of the fetus or infant assaults the assumptions of each parent, assumptions about the orderliness of the world and the goodness of the parent. Each parent uses various coping mechanisms in an effort to deal emotionally with the loss.

In Chapter 4, the destabilization of the couple relationship is explored. Usually, fetal or infant death places considerable strain on the marriage, as both partners attempt to deal with their own grief while contending also with their partner's feelings and the reactions of outsiders. Each spouse has expectations of the other spouse, which are rarely wholly met by the other. In Chapter 5, the restabilization of the couple relationship is examined. Sooner or later, most of our respondents found ways to deal with their conflicting expectations and incongruent grieving. Here, marital communication, a positive view, the ability to reframe their experience, and flexibility were some of the strengths that helped couples to cope with their shared loss.

The loss experience is framed in Chapter 6 in terms of gender roles. In a time of crisis, people fall back upon habits and familiar patterns of behavior. Because this loss involves their identity as a mother or father, many bereaved parents talk about their experiences in terms of their expectations for themselves as women and men. Seeing oneself as performing adequately as a woman or man seems to help bereaved parents to form a healing theory.

Chapter 7 examines the social support that our respondents received as individuals and as couples. All persons with whom they had contact following their loss were potential sources of help or distress. Because medical personnel are "on the front lines," their responses have particular importance. Medical personnel can provide valuable information to newly bereaved parents that will help them to cope with their feelings and with other people. Other sources of support, positive and negative, include members of the clergy, colleagues and bosses, and friends and family members.

Chapter 8 explores the kind of help that our respondents said that bereaved parents need, and gives suggestions for helping professionals based on the findings of our study.

In Chapter 9, Britton Wood, a practicing family therapist and grief counselor, applies the results of our study to therapeutic intervention for married couples who have experienced pregnancy loss or infant death. Taking a pragmatic approach, chapters 2 through 8 are outlined concisely for the benefit of helping professionals who may wish to self-brief prior to a therapy session. In addition, specific intervention tools, based on the information presented in the book, are included.

2

Parental Grief Resolution at Two Levels

An Introduction

Dr. Jones told us that 9 out of 10 marriages break up from the death of a child. [Melanie]

We have a choice. Danny's death can make us stronger, or it can tear us apart. [One of the authors to her husband, following the fetal death of their son]

For newly bereaved parents, there are many unknown factors. The unexpected death of their baby; the unanticipated reactions of their family members, friends, and colleagues and perhaps each other; and worry about marital conflict, and perhaps even divorce, overwhelm the parents. There is no doubt that stressor events such as the illness or death of a child, unemployment, or disasters like earthquakes place a strain on a marriage. But misinformation such as that received by Melanie from her physician only adds to the feelings of stress. It *would* help Melanie to know that increased marital conflict is likely, and that spouses usually have different styles of grieving.

Our goal is to describe the grief reactions of married couples who experienced pregnancy loss or infant death. Although we recognize that not all newly bereaved parents are married and that some couples *do* divorce following such an experience, it is our hope that by examining intact couples, something can be learned about the way that married pairs negotiate the rocky shores of bereavement.

After the death of a child, both parents grieve. Both partners must struggle with their own loss while attempting to cope with changes in the other and their relationship. In order to understand the particular problems that result from such a complex situation, the grief process must be examined at both the *individual* and the *couple* levels. Parental grief resolution occurs at both levels simultaneously, and when change during the grief process occurs at one level, it influences the other.

Grieving, whether conceptualized as an individual or a couple process, takes place within the context of a social ecology. Extended family members, friends, neighbors, bosses, colleagues, members of the couple's church or temple, and acquaintances all react to the news of the infant's death and to the reactions of the bereaved couple. These individuals and groups may provide social support that is helpful, harmful, or a combination of both, thus easing the painful transition or making it more painful. Social customs may exist that are understood by all members of the social group, or by only some of them, or there may be a lack of shared understanding about what one does when an infant dies. Unfortunately, in the case of infant death, and particularly pregnancy loss, there are few mutually understood social rituals to aid the bereaved.

In general, grief resolution has been explored as an individual response with little attention paid to family processes (Raphael, 1983). Parental grief is no exception. Indeed, not only has the emphasis been on the individual, it has been primarily on the mother. Little attention has been given to the father or to the impact of the loss on the couple's relationship.

Yet, in discussing family response to child loss, Bowlby (1980) has suggested that successful completion of the parental grief process requires that parents grieve in tandem. That is, both partners must grieve together and provide support and comfort to one another. If they don't, Bowlby believes that the marriage and the emotional state of each partner is placed at risk. Although such a mutual grief experience is the ideal, incongruent (Peppers & Knapp, 1980b) or dissimilar grief appears to be the norm. As will be detailed in Chapter 4, incongruent grief was the most common form of interactive grief found in this study. As expected, respondents indicated that their expectation that they would grieve in the same way, having experienced the same loss, contributed to increased tension in a majority of the marriages. Yet, as will be described in Chapter 5, our data indicate that couples' acceptance of the differences inherent in their grief styles and their ability to take a positive view of these differences may serve to strengthen the marriage.

Information presented here is directed primarily to readers unfamiliar with the grief and family trauma literature. Those familiar with these areas may wish to skip to the third chapter, where we begin to report on the results of our study.

Before examining the experience of dyadic (couple) grief, we will briefly review prior writings on individual grief process and the process of resolution of trauma and loss in a family. In describing the grieving process, we will refer to grief, mourning, and grief work. These terms have been used in a variety of ways to define different aspects of the response to the loss of a loved one. Here, *grief* is seen as the emotional, physiological, and behavioral reactions resulting from the loss of a significant other.

Mourning has been defined in two very different ways. It has been used in psychoanalytic theory to describe the same psychological processes that we have defined as grief. The term has also been used to define the public expression of grief. Seen in this context, the extent to which one may and may not publicly express grief is restricted by cultural prescriptions and sanctions and, more directly, by the censure of members of the individual's social networks. In this text, we have chosen to use the second definition, that of mourning as the public, socially constrained behavioral response to a loss.

Grief work encompasses both grief and mourning. The purpose of bereavement is to ameliorate the often painful thoughts and emotions connected to the loss (Lindenmann, 1944).

In the following sections, several of the more familiar stage models of grief will be reviewed. Most of these stage models consider grief at only the individual level. Then, several process models will be examined. Following these, stage and process models of family response will be presented.

GRIEF AS A SERIES OF STAGES

The process of grief resolution most often has been conceptualized as a series of stages or phases through which the bereaved must work in order to resolve their grief successfully (Kübler-Ross, 1969). These stage models are popular among laypersons and professionals alike.

The Parkes/Bowlby Model

Parkes (1972) and Bowlby (1980) have proposed similar models of the grief process, which follow a pattern of distinctly discernible phases through which the bereaved must pass in order to resolve their grief. The four phases are:

NUMBING

This phase usually lasts a few hours to a week. At this point, the bereaved is stunned and unable to accept the reality of the death. This sense of unreality may be interrupted by anger outbursts or panic attacks.

YEARNING AND SEARCHING

In this phase, which is believed to last months or even years, the urge to recover and be reunited with the deceased is strong. As the loss becomes more real, intense pining replaces the numbness of the first phase. There may be preoccupation with the deceased. At the same time, the bereaved may hallucinate and "sense" the presence of the deceased and may fear "going crazy." Memories of the deceased are quite vivid. Anger episodes, associated with yearning, are interspersed with episodes of depressive withdrawal, associated with despair. The bereaved may consider suicide during this time. Efforts will be made to find someone or something to blame to answer the "Why me?" question.

DISORGANIZATION AND DESPAIR

At this time, the finality of the loss is recognized. Efforts to retain a connection with the deceased are seen as pointless.

REORGANIZATION AND RECOVERY

Old patterns of acting, feeling, and thinking may be abandoned at this time. A "redefinition of the self" takes place as the bereaved sees himself or herself as separate from the deceased. The bereaved begins to see the world in a more positive light.

Throughout this grief resolution process, individuals may oscillate between any two phases. Over time, however, an overall pattern of movement through these phases should be discerned (Bowlby, 1980).

KÜBLER-ROSS MODEL

Perhaps the most popular stage model of grief is Kübler-Ross's five-stage model (1969). She suggested that both the dying and the bereaved experience a series of stages as they adjust to the reality of death. These stages include (1) denial and isolation, (2) anger, (3) bargaining, (4) depression, and, finally, (5) acceptance. The bereaved are assumed to move through these stages in order to come to a successful resolution of their loss.

Such stage or phase models of grief resolution have been used widely in investigations of parental grief (cf. Edelstein,

1984; Frantz, 1984; Miles, 1984; Peppers & Knapp, 1980b). Although they contain some minor variations, the overall structure of stage models of parental grief is in agreement with those presented above. That is, they assume a period of disorganization, followed by a time of emotional extremes and cognitive dissonance, completed by a resolution of the loss.

STAGE MODELS OF FAMILY ADAPTATION

As with individual grief, stage models have been suggested for family adaptation processes. Hill (1949, 1958) identified a pattern similar to the stage/phase models of Bowlby (1980) and Parkes (1972) that he termed a "roller-coaster" profile of adjustment for families. In this view, families move from a relatively stable *precrisis* state into the crisis, which precipitates a period of *disorganization*. This period is followed by a *reaction and reorganization* on the part of the family, which then leads to *readjustment and recovery*. The level of final readjustment and recovery is positively related to two factors: *integration* is seen as the coherent unity and sense of interdependence within the family; *adaptability* is the amount of flexibility of the family unit.

McCubbin and Patterson's Family Adjustment and Adaptation Response (FAAR) Model

McCubbin and Patterson (1983) also proposed a stage model of adaptation. This model involves the following stages:

FAMILY RESISTANCE

Initially, many families are seen to focus on maintaining the situation as it was before the crisis, using the same coping strategies as before. Eventually, they come to realize that they must begin to change. Family members often resist change. When this occurs, an increase of stress, or "pileup," may result.

FAMILY RESTRUCTURING

Family structure is often changed to fit the altered picture of family membership. The family may become disorganized by the change, with minimal indications of coherent family functioning.

FAMILY CONSOLIDATION

Because of disorganization and incoherence, additional changes are then made in the family in order to restore stability. The "family perception of the event" or the meaning that the family gives to the event (e.g., "It was God's will") is arrived at through negotiation and compromise.

REASSESSING THE STAGE/PHASE MODELS

Although stage models would seem to fit the progression of normal grief, little evidence exists to support them. In an extensive review of the literature, Silver and Wortman (1980) were unable to find any evidence that individuals went through a series of stages following a traumatic event. Indeed, grief does not appear to be tied to a fixed order of emotional states. Rather, it appears to be related to the closeness of the relationship with the deceased and the perception of preventability of the death (Bugan, 1983; Wortman & Silver, 1989). Alternatively, emotions and behaviors that have been described as aspects of grief phases by Bowlby may be simultaneously present, with each becoming more apparent during the course of recovery (Davidson, 1979).

Another problem with a stage/phase model is the assumption that, for most victims, there will be a resolution of grief. There is increasing evidence that this may not be true (Silver & Wortman, 1980; Wortman & Silver, 1989).

In particular, parental grief does not appear to follow stages. Rando (1983) was unable to find evidence that parents of children who died from cancer moved through stages of recovery. Instead of a steady improvement of their functioning, these parents showed signs of increasing grief 3 years after the death of their child. Grief for these parents seemed to worsen with time. The same pattern of worsening grief over time was found to be true for parents of homicide victims (Rinear, 1984).

Frantz (1984) identified a more complicated pattern of parental grieving in which parents experienced an increase in intensity between 6 and 12 months after the child's death. Complicating the situation is the fact that parents assumed their grief would lessen with time. Instead, they suffered from recurring, intrusive thoughts about their child. As a result, many expressed their fear that they were "going crazy." Thus, their inability to match the pattern of their own experience with the anticipated stages of grief appears to have compounded the negative effects of the loss.

Stage and phase models of family stress have also been criticized as unrealistic and unrepresentative of actual family processes. Families do not appear to recover from a traumatic experience as a unit in an orderly chain of stages. Rather, what have been described as stages overlap and individuals influence one another, resulting in a more complex and disorderly sequence of events than stage theorists suggest (Reiss, 1981).

PROCESS MODELS OF GRIEF RESOLUTION

Parkes (1972) has proposed that grief is the response of the bereaved to the destruction of all that is meaningful in their world. He speaks of the destruction of the *assumptive world*, a generalized set of beliefs within which the individual operates on a day-to-day basis. This belief structure allows one to organize information encountered in the environment and to reasonably anticipate future events. According to Parkes, the central task of bereavement is to fit the loss into the assumptions or to modify the assumptions so that the loss may be accepted as real. This assumptive world, "developed and confirmed over many years, cannot account for these extreme events. The old assumptions and theories of reality are shattered, producing psychological upheaval" (Janoff-Bulman, 1985, p. 18).

Other scholars have expressed similar views: Grief has been seen as the *loss of meaning* and bereavement as the process of reconstructing the generalized belief structure (Marris, 1982). Finally, Hoagland (1984) has proposed, in her *personal construct theory of bereavement*, that the bereaved must create their own theory to explain the loss while they integrate the reality of the death into their worldview. The overall view is of grief as an effort to make sense of the loss.

This "making sense of the loss" sounds deceptively simple. It is, in fact, quite difficult because it requires the bereaved to restructure their perception of reality in order to come to terms with the death. Throughout this process, bereaved persons are often in a state of confusion, with little opportunity to register a clear mental picture. The result is that the images of the event are fragmented and disjointed, and attributing meaning to these images becomes difficult (Horowitz, 1986; Janoff-Bulman, 1985; Loftus, 1979).

Grief, then, is not simply a response to the absence of the person who died. Rather, it is the reaction to the disintegration of the whole world of meaning dependent on the relationship with that person. According to Rowe (1982), "The individual world of meaning is a complicated, interconnected network of meanings that encompasses not only present relationships with people and things but past and the future" (p. 14).

DEVELOPING A PERSONAL THEORY

In order to recover from a loss, the bereaved must attribute meaning to it, and some sort of explanation, a personal or "healing" theory, must be developed (Figley, 1983, 1985; Taylor, Lichtman, & Wood, 1987). This is done by their answering such questions about the loss as what happened, how it happened, why it happened to them, why they responded as they did, and what they would do if it happened again (Figley, 1983). According to Figley, the specific questions asked are not as important as the answers, that is, the meaning given to the event. By constructing such a healing theory, the bereaved modify the assumptive world to incorporate the loss, thereby achieving a new sense of normalcy and purpose. In this way, they are able to reestablish the sense of control and predictability felt prior to the event, finding some sort of understanding and gaining a sense of mastery with regard to the event (Taylor, 1983).

After a loss, bereaved parents report being told to "get on with your life" or "get back to normal." They may find it difficult to do this because their lives have become, in a very real sense, meaningless, and there is nothing they can call "normal."

> Losing someone you love is less like losing a very valuable and irreplaceable possession than like finding the law of gravity to be invalid. . . . But, however it is achieved, the recovery from a sense of loss seems to depend on restoring the continuity of meaning. (Marris, 1982, pp. 195–196)

Forming a Healing Theory and Parental Assumptions

In the case of parental bereavement, the initial belief system includes the unique meaning the child holds for each parent. As this varies greatly from parent to parent, the impact of the loss varies among parents. Elements of the assumptive world directly affected include what the child symbolizes for each parent, the importance of the parent role, the unnaturalness of a child's predeceasing the parent, and the response of the support network (Rando, 1984). In addition to the variety of assumptions, the intensity with which the parents hold these assumptions and the fact that they must be faced over and over again after the child's death can have an effect on the dyadic grief process.

GRIEF AND THE NEED FOR CLOSURE

Throughout the grief process, the bereaved must cope with preoccupation with thoughts of the lost person, and a strong urge to recover and reunite with that person, as well as with painful recollections of the loss experience. Raphael (1983) has suggested that these repetitive, intrusive images of the loss and the resultant strong emotions fit the model for a stress response syndrome centering on the integration of disturbing memories. As noted previously, there is a strong urge to integrate the new information about the event with the existent assumptive world. Horowitz (1976, 1979, 1986) has proposed that this compulsion to define the event is powered by the *completion tendency,* a drive to integrate new information with one's existing assumptive world and to establish consistency between old and new schema. Until this consistency is established, intrusive thoughts about the loss will recur (Horowitz, 1982). At the same time, these thoughts are often painful and the bereaved may attempt to suppress them. The end result is an unstable conflict between intrusive images and avoidant behavior, which will continue until the loss has been integrated and closure has been achieved (Horowitz, 1976).

Parents have reported such recurrences of intense grief long after the death of their child. In one study, Rinear (1984) reported that, for grieving parents of homicide victims, vivid, painful memories, which she termed "aftershocks," were present an average of 3 years after their child had been murdered. A similar phenomenon occurs for persons who have experienced fetal or infant loss in that they reported experiencing transitory recurrences of grief sensations (Peppers & Knapp, 1980b). This *shadow grief* was not as intense as the grief of those parents described above, but as long-term grieving had not been anticipated following a loss so early in life, this was surprising to the parents who experienced it.

In a study of long-term effects of fetal/infant loss, Rosenblatt and Burns (1986) also found that almost 25% of parents who had lost a child during pregnancy or early infancy experienced occasional or frequent pangs of grief. In addition, some of these pangs were described as intense, even though the time since death ranged from 2 to 46 years.

Wortman and Silver (1989) have examined what they call a myth that is held by many clinicians that there is a normal process of recovery from irrevocable loss. They maintain that an intense initial reaction does not predict a good recovery. For example, some parents react mildly to the death of a child and eventually recover; others feel various levels of grief for many years. In particular they criticize persons influenced by psychoanalytic thought who believe that grief must be "worked through." This pattern is typical of some, but not all of the bereaved, and is not more "healthy" than either of the other two patterns (a consistently mild reaction or a consistently virulent one).

PROCESS MODELS OF FAMILY STRESS ADAPTATION

The destruction of meaning may also be important to grief resolution at the couple level. Reiss and Oliveri (1980) have suggested that families share a set of beliefs, assumptions, and orientations, which they call a *family paradigm*. This concept is very similar to Parkes' (1976) assumptive world. Individual and couple views of reality are developed in a social environment. Over time, couples develop a shared way of perceiving the world (Berger & Kellner, 1964; Reiss, 1981). When a major event occurs in a family, families are believed to use their family paradigm to create a *family definition of the event* (Hill, 1949) or *family perception of the event* (McCubbin & Patterson, 1983).

The family paradigm is far more complex than the individual's assumptive world, encompassing each individual family member's perceptions as well as expectations and perceptions of each other. The family paradigm is not seen as a unitary view of the situation. Rather, the emphasis is on the closeness of the family members' views of the situation and their ability to work as a problem-solving team. Such a paradigm is continually being modified and built upon, and one source of problems for couples losing a child, especially early in their marriage, is that they may not have had an opportunity to develop a paradigm that would incorporate appropriate family response to such an event.

Use of the family paradigm model to study dyadic response to loss is somewhat problematic in that the family paradigm has been applied to family organization only during normative transitions, which are expected transitional events, such as the birth of a baby, a child going to kindergarten or first grade, the marriage of the young adult child, or the death of the aged parent. Although somewhat stressful, the expectedness of the transition provides family members with prior knowledge of it and with appropriate responses to it.

Reiss and Oliveri (1980) have suggested that the family paradigm may disintegrate in the face of such traumatic events as an untimely death in the family. The fact that this may occur allows this model to be consistent with models that detail the impact of loss on the individual's assumptive world. The assumptive worlds of individual family members are being assaulted by the death of a loved one, and interactional patterns based on these assumptions can no longer be maintained. It is possible that this is the source of many of the difficulties in the family following the death of a child. Thus, contrary to the suggestions of its original authors, the fact that the family paradigm may collapse in the face of catastrophe is, in a sense, a strength of this model.

Figley (1989) has proposed that the family forms a *family healing theory* after a catastrophic event:

> a set of statements about the circumstances under which the traumatic event happened, how and why each family member behaved as they did (during and following the event), and an optimistic scenario of what would happen if a similar traumatic event took place again. (Figley, 1989, p. 98)

In a process similar to but more complex than the formation of a personal healing theory, Figley suggests that each person answers questions about the event regarding himself or herself and other family members. In this process, family members exchange information about the event related to their personal healing theories. These personal healing theories eventually coalesce into a single, unifying family healing theory that explains the event and the behavior of family members in relation to the event. As the personal healing theory fits into the new, modified assumptive world of the individual, the family healing theory fits into the new, modified family paradigm.

In summary, the parental grief process has been explored from a number of perspectives. The validity of stage models is questionable. The most promising alternative view is a more fluid model in which the assumptive world is reconstructed to include information related to the death. This approach accounts for persons who experience periods of recurrent grief episodes and the difficulty in giving up images associated with the deceased. This model also suggests a need for a healing theory to make sense of a loss experience, regardless of the age of the person who has died.

As with grief on a personal level, the family's response to highly stressful situations, such as the death of a family member, has been suggested to follow a stage model. In addition, the concept of family paradigm can be seen as very similar to that of personal assumptive world. A possible extension of this paradigm model is the family healing theory, or a unifying explanation of the event shared by all family members.

SOCIAL SUPPORT AND THE RECONSTRUCTION OF MEANING

After the death of their child, parents' efforts at redefinition and explanation are legitimized through interaction with others (Berger & Luckman, 1966; Holzner, 1968). In our culture, marriage is held to be the primary source of social support for married adults in the United States (Blood & Wolfe, 1960; Burke & Weir, 1977). According to Burke and Weir (1982), "There are very few dyadic relationships in our society that provide individuals with the degree of proximity, accessibility, commitment, interdependence, and opportunity for intimacy that marriage does" (p. 221).

Thus, marital partners hold a unique position in legitimizing one another's beliefs and perceptions (Berger & Kellner, 1964). Bowlby (1980) believes that this characteristic of modern marriage has pressing implications for bereaved parents:

> How well or badly mourning proceeds . . . turns in great degree on the parents' own relationship. When they can mourn together, keep in step from one phase to the next, each deriving comfort and support from the other, the outcome of their mourning is favorable. When, by contrast, the parents are in conflict and mutual support absent, the family may break up and/or individual family members become psychiatric casualties. [pp. 120–121]

However, whether or not this is actually the case for most couples following bereavement has not been explored. The prior literature on formation of a family paradigm has examined only noncrisis situations (Reiss, 1981).

In their daily interactions, spouses are able to consider and validate each other's view of what has happened, is happening, and will happen (Berger & Kellner, 1964; Reiss, 1981). As they work to make sense of their experience, each compares and attempts to confirm beliefs, opinions, hunches, and healing theories with the other. If they confirm one another's subjective views of each other, these views are given objective reality; that is, what they perceive comes to be seen as reality because significant others also see it that way (Berger & Luckman, 1966; Holzner, 1968); if not, they question their own or the other's perceptions, and formation of an objective reality is made more difficult.

McCubbin and Patterson (1983) proposed that perceptions of

a stressor event change over time as resources are gathered and utilized and as coping occurs. Mutual confirmation of views contributes to a perception that stability and control have returned. The new information resulting from the catastrophic experience is incorporated into the assumptive world and begins to contribute to its ability to organize and predict day-to-day experience. In addition, mutually validated definitions facilitate communication, provide structure and meaning to their interactions, and serve as the basis for dyadic coping behavior (McCubbin & Patterson, 1983; Reiss, 1981; Reiss & Oliveri, 1980).

Thus, bereaved parents often turn to each other for comfort, support, and confirmation of the legitimacy of their feelings of loss (Rosenblatt & Burns, 1986; Schiff, 1977). If this is available, it may, in fact, be the best source of support. Helmrath and Steinitz (1978) found that sharing of feelings between marital partners and the resulting mutual trust proved to be the most important factor to the resolution of their grief.

An examination of the literature suggests that bereaved parents are not always able to provide each other with this support and comfort (cf. Borg & Lasker, 1989; Frantz, 1984; Munson, 1978; Peppers & Knapp, 1980b; Rando, 1983, 1984; Schiff, 1977). Parents have said that, in addition to losing the child, they felt they had lost their spouse for a time (Rando, 1983), or that their spouse was often the least helpful person in coping with the death (Frantz, 1984; Schiff, 1977).

Specific problems related to support exist for fetal and infant death. For example, the need for confirmation of the reality of the loss is particularly important (Rosenblatt & Burns, 1986). Faced with a support network that refuses to acknowledge that the bereaved parents have a legitimate claim to their grief, parents who have experienced such a loss may turn to each other for this confirmation. Spouses may not be able to provide support at a time at which they are under intense pressure themselves. Because of their unique relationship with their baby and their idiosyncratic coping style, each spouse's resultant need to discuss and work through the loss may be quite different from the other's. A spouse who has a different grieving style may not wish to dwell on the death. Or one spouse simply may not have experienced the loss to be as painful as the other has.

THE COUPLE AND GRIEF

Several different processes are occurring simultaneously as parents attempt to come to grips with their loss. Intense emotions may be experienced as the reality of a future without this child is faced, accepted, and integrated into their assumptive world. The symbolic significance of the loss is different for each parent. As a result, they do not experience the same emotional reactions to the loss. In addition, inconsistencies in both short- and long-term grief reactions may exist between spouses. The interaction of these differences and related conflicts may come together to place tremendous stress and strain on the marital dyad.

Indeed, the picture presented in the literature is one of parents experiencing a great deal of difficulty in the grief process. They have described feeling a sense of unreality in their child's predeceasing them (Halpern, 1983; Rando, 1984), feeling a loss of control (Arnold & Gemma, 1983), fearing "going crazy" (Frantz, 1984), and believing that their future has been lost (Schiff, 1977). They may express inappropriate guilt at the death (Borg & Lasker, 1989; Schiff, 1977), or they may blame each other (Rando, 1984; Schiff, 1977). Mothers are more prone to feelings of guilt at the death of a child in pregnancy or infancy. Peppers and Knapp (1980a,b) found this to be especially true for women who experienced miscarriages.

Overprotection and Isolation

Because of the obvious pain involved in discussions of the death, spouses may attempt to overprotect one another (Cornwell, Nurcombe, & Stevens, 1977; Munson, 1978; Schiff, 1977). Weitzman and Kamm (1985) have found that this over-protectiveness diminishes the ability to communicate, and effective communication has been shown to be essential to successful dyadic functioning (Epstein & Westley, 1959; Figley, 1983). Therefore, by avoiding discussions of their loss, they may cause one another to feel isolated and without support.

Differences in the Symbolic Loss

In addition, although both partners experienced the same objective loss, what the child symbolized to each of them may be extremely different, leading to different grief experiences, and perhaps therefore to conflict (Arnold & Gemma, 1983; Rando, 1984). In addition, the ambiguity at fetal/infant loss, especially early in the pregnancy, can lead to sharply different assessments of exactly what has been lost (Rosenblatt & Burns, 1986).

Incongruent Grieving

Conflicts may result because parents expect one another to grieve in a manner consistent with their own grief (Miles, 1984). This incongruence (Peppers & Knapp, 1980b) or lack of synchronicity in grieving (Miles, 1984; Rando, 1980, 1983; Osterweis, Solomon, & Green, 1984) also contributes to a sense of isolation in the marriage (Munson, 1978).

Men have been reported to be more likely to avoid going through the grieving process than women (Frantz, 1984). Osterweis et al. (1984) found that fathers experienced their most intense grieving within the first few weeks to 1 month, while the mothers' grief extended over a longer period of time. Emotions were different, with mothers feeling more sorrow and depression and fathers feeling more anger, fear, and loss of control.

Incongruent grieving has been documented for grief associated with fetal/infant loss. In their study of maternal grieving at miscarriage, stillbirth, or neonatal loss, Peppers and Knapp

(1980a) found a great deal of similarity in the intensity of mothers' acute grief, regardless of the type of fetal/infant loss. In a related report, they stated that paternal grieving, as reported by the women who participated in the study, was very specific and individualized (Pepper & Knapp, 1980b). The authors suggested that this was due to incongruent bonding with the child on the parts of mothers and fathers, with the mother bonding during the pregnancy while the father does not do so until after the child's birth.*

Cornwell et al. (1977) interviewed members of 17 families that had experienced the loss of a child from Sudden Infant Death Syndrome (SIDS) and found that the father's grief was less intense and was resolved much sooner than the mother's. The subjective assessment of participants was that an average of 10.3 months for the women and 3.6 months for the men passed before they were able to resume normal functioning. Regardless of the differences in grieving, however, these researchers also found a sort of "resonating grief," in which one of the parents would express strong emotions, such as weeping, and the other would respond similarly.

Mandell, McAnulty, and Reece (1980), in a fetal/infant death study focusing on fathers, found distinctly different patterns of response to the death of a child from SIDS. Fathers took on a managerial role, intellectualized their emotions, increased their involvement outside the home, and expressed a strong desire for future children. All of these characteristics were in sharp contrast to the grief response of their wives. Benefield, Lieb, and Vollman (1978) and Helmrath and Steinitz (1978) found that maternal grief significantly exceeded paternal grief. In addition, Helmrath and Steinitz found that the character of the wives' grief was different from their husbands', with men

---

*These findings must be viewed with caution, as the authors interviewed only women and asked them about their own and their husband's grief. On the basis of the inconsistency that we observed in this study between the intent of one spouse's behavior and the interpretation by the other, we must question the accuracy of the findings. It is possible that the differences in grieving were more a function of the contrast between expectations and observation on the part of the wives than of actual behavior on the part of the husbands.

limiting their show of grief to a greater extent because of the belief that society expected them to be strong for their wives.

Additional Stressors

Compounding the problem, parents may have to cope with other stressors, such as financial difficulties, if the child had been hospitalized (Schiff, 1977). Parenting of remaining children can act as a stressor, especially if the children are old enough to ask about the missing sibling (Borg & Lasker, 1989; Rando, 1984).

In addition to these internal problems that the couple experiences, they are often unable to mourn publicly. Bereaved parents have reported feeling stigmatized and shunned (Arnold & Gemma, 1983; Frantz, 1984; Getzel & Masters, 1984; Helmrath & Steinitz, 1978; Schiff, 1977). The social environment isolates the couple so that they must do their grieving in private (Stephenson, 1985).

In addition, there is a general lack of consensus as to a proper mourning period. Davidson (1979) discussed a "man in the street" poll in which an overwhelming number of respondents stated a belief that between 48 hours and 2 weeks was a normal and appropriate mourning period. This conclusion contrasted sharply with the findings of his study that indicated that adults took an average of 18 to 24 months to complete the grieving process. With fetal/infant loss, the ambiguity regarding mourning is even more pronounced (Davidson, 1979; Rosenblatt & Burns, 1986). There is a lack of understanding of the need to mourn the death of a child who many may not have considered to be a person (Helmrath & Steinitz, 1978).

In summary, the marital relationship is often seen as a primary source of social support and comfort for partners. Yet, when faced with the death of their child, although it is natural that the partners turn to each other for this support and comfort, they may not be able to do so. Couples may attempt to discuss the death with one another but because of mismatched needs, they may not be able to do so. There is a great potential for conflict in the marital couple from a variety of sources: Differences in meanings of the death, grief style, expectations for each other, and difficulties in coping with strong emotions are several ways in which these conflicts may occur. In addition, external pressures, such as financial strain or the feeling of being stigmatized by others, can add to the burden of the couple.

CONCLUSION

Following the fetal or infant death of a child, both spouses experience changes as they grieve the death of their child. In addition, changes occur in their marital relationship. These have been explored using stage models as well as process models of individual grief and family system adaptation. As an effort to confront the devastation of the assumptive world, grief is seen as the work of reconstructing a new assumptive world. In Chapter 3, we will explore the process through which bereaved parents move in their efforts to integrate the death of their child into their assumptive worlds. An important element in these efforts is the support network that serves to validate and confirm the modified assumptive world of the bereaved parents. The view of the spouse is of critical importance in this regard. As shown in Chapter 4, because of their unique grief experience and the intensity of their own suffering, spouses are not always the best choice as supporter at this time.

Other members of their support network also are seen as resources at this time. Again, our findings suggest that these supporters may be of limited use, as they may lack the necessary sensitivity to assist the bereaved parents in their efforts to reconstruct their shattered assumptive world. In the following chapters, we will show how our respondent couples dealt with their loss and coped with the "second wound" (Symonds, 1980) of rejection and insensitivity of their supporters, while also attempting to deal with the impact of the loss on their relationship.

3

Grief on the
Individual Level

The Grieving Process

This chapter and the following two chapters describe the response of parents to the death of their child. This chapter explores the subjective experience of parents as individuals, and the following two chapters explore the complexity of two people coping with the loss of their child while attempting to meet their responsibilities as members of a marital dyad.

When their child died, the parents in our study found themselves confused and disoriented. Making no sense, the death disrupted their perception of order and meaning in their lives.

I just couldn't believe it happened . . . [I was] just trying to get my mind to accept what had really happened. I didn't want to . . . believe it had really happened. [Peter]

Viewed globally, the grieving did appear to approximate the stage model. However, when examined in relation to individual parents, grieving approximated overlapping *phases* rather than clear-cut stages.* We suggest a model similar to Davidson's

*The controversy over whether stages or phases exist can be resolved by considering the methodology that is used. When considered by averaging a large number of cases with the goal of a global picture, there do appear to be phases. When considered in detail, however, an individual

(Davidson, 1979), which proposed that various aspects of the grief process are present simultaneously. During the course of grief resolution, the various aspects wax and wane in importance. In addition, we found that not all respondents achieved the same degree of resolution of grief and reconstruction of their assumptive world.

The grief process generally began with disorientation and confusion, followed by the parents' efforts to adapt to and deal with the conflict between their extant assumptive world and the information presented by their baby's death. Finally, the assumptive world was reconstructed to incorporate at least some elements of the reality of their baby's death. The process of grieving was highly individualized, and in virtually all of the couples, the course of each partner's grief was different from the other partner's. What follows here is a synthesis of their grief resolution. As indicated above, these are not phases or stages that occur in a sequential order but a set of processes that often overlap and recur as parents attempt to come to terms with the death of their child.

INITIAL IMPACT: DISRUPTION OF THE ASSUMPTIVE WORLD

Assumptions Assaulted

As discussed in the previous chapter, Janoff-Bulman (1985) suggests that individuals who have experienced a catastrophe must deal with the impact of that event on a number of assumptions. In general, participants in this study faced the disruption of these assumptions: the meaning of the child for them, both as a person and as a part of themselves; a belief in personal invulnerability, both for themselves and their child; a positive view of themselves and their child; and the belief in an orderly

---

does not appear to go through distinct stages. However, people who have been taught to do so may perceive stages when looking back upon a series of events.

world that is both predictable and meaningful. These assumptions are interrelated and affect one another. They are separated here for the purpose of clarification.

THE MEANING OF THE CHILD

As they look forward to the birth of their child, prospective parents construct an image of and bond with their child during pregnancy (Klauss & Kennel, 1976). Women, in particular, begin to construct such an image early in the pregnancy (Borg & Lasker, 1989; Peppers & Knapp, 1980b); some women in this study felt an attachment to an imagined child even before the start of the pregnancy. This was particularly apparent in the two cases of early fetal death that occurred before the mother began to "show." As Phillip said of his wife, Linda, following the loss of their first child in the 13th week of her pregnancy:

It's partly because Linda wanted to have a baby when we got married, almost 5 years ago. . . . I really think the attachment with Linda grew, on the child, even before the pregnancy ever started.

Possibly because of this early attachment, women expressed their reaction to the death of their child in terms of a wound to or a loss of a part of themselves: "I thought I'd die of a broken heart," and "It was like someone took a part of my very soul."

The self-image of our respondents began to include a picture of themselves as parents. With the death of their child, they lost the basis for this image, but not the image itself. This may be particularly painful for those who have no living children. When he advised other bereaved fathers, Henry spoke of his wife's perception of herself as a mother after they had experienced their third pregnancy loss:

For Mother's Day, get her a present because she really is a mother. And everybody says, "The baby wasn't born alive, so is she really a mother?" But for 20 bucks go get her a present.

PERSONAL INVULNERABILITY

The most common assumptive statements centered on an assumption of invulnerability to harm. Prior to their child's death, these individuals may have accepted the abstract concept that children die; it was frequently mentioned, however, that these sorts of things happen to other people, not themselves. The possibility that such a terrible event would befall them was unthinkable.

It seems like you read all these things happening but you never thought it would happen to you, as far as losing a child. [Willa]

A number of men and women also expressed a related belief that, since they were protected, their child would be protected as well. A family history of safety might be seen as evidence of this protection:

And [my husband] was worried and I said, "Hey what's to worry about? Nothing ever happens like this. . . . Nobody's ever sick in our family. They live forever," I said. Well, well, well. [Miriam]

A POSITIVE VIEW OF ONESELF AND ONE'S CHILD

This assumption was closely related to the view of personal invulnerability. These individuals saw themselves as basically good people who deserved to be rewarded for their goodness. Prior to the death of their child, many viewed the world as a fair and just place in which each person somehow is "paid back" for all transgressions. Often it was this perception of themselves as good people that served as the basis for seeing themselves as invulnerable. Diane spoke for many of these parents when she described her response to the news that her newborn daughter would die: "I thought, 'Oh, this isn't true, bad things don't happen to good people.'"

Their positive view of themselves frequently was extended to the baby. Even those persons who might have accepted that they somehow might have deserved to be punished believed that the innate goodness and innocence of the baby would protect him or her. Melissa's son was born prematurely and died 10 hours after birth, and she expressed her beliefs about him in this way:

> Maybe I've been bad and I'm being punished but you can't tell me that child was bad. Why was that child punished? Why did he have to suffer? He was an innocent little baby. He didn't live long enough to get into any kind of trouble or do anything intentionally wrong.

THE BELIEF IN AN ORDERLY WORLD

An essential aspect of the assumption of an orderly world is the belief in cause and effect (Janoff-Bulman, 1985). For many parents, this need to believe that some medical cause could be identified led to frustration with their physician or the medical establishment. (This problem was especially apparent for parents who had experienced a fetal death.) When viewed from a religious or philosophical perspective, the apparent randomness, the lack of "fairness," of the death seemed cruel and arbitrary. "We could offer [a child] so much. It's not fair at all."

Parents who had experienced a previous loss or some other family crisis also felt that the loss of their baby was unfair. They expressed the belief that "the price had been paid" and that "there was enough suffering in our family." Now, it should be someone else's turn to suffer.

In order to function in the present and plan for the future, one necessarily sees the world as predictable and orderly. In such a just world, one can plan carefully and take precautions in order to exert some control in the future. The impact of the death on this assumption was one of tremendous confusion and frustration. After he had experienced the second fetal death of a child, Nick expressed the following sentiment:

> I didn't know what to do. I felt confused, frustrated. Here I was a smart person, and I couldn't figure out how to get something.

Finally, many of the women in the study expressed shock and amazement that, regardless of what they did during pregnancy, the outcome was completely beyond their control. The realization that other women were careless about their prenatal care and had "perfect babies" or did not marry or abused their children but were able to "pop out babies left and right" was especially incomprehensible. During the interview, it was common for them to give detailed descriptions of their efforts to assure their pregnancy's success.

THE IMPACT OF THE LOSS

Initially, as has been shown in other research on threats to children (Chodoff, Friedman, & Hamburg, 1964), parents are stunned by their loss. Terms like "weird," "strange," and "unreal" were used by our respondents to describe the situation in which they found themselves. They varied in the speed with which they came to realize the seriousness of the situation. Each of them described an initial sense of confusion. As suggested by Parkes (1976), they could not understand what had happened and felt numb and "out of synch." The sense of being overwhelmed by the changed reality may have been related to receiving more information than they could take in. Overwhelmed, they simply shut down.

The initial impact was described as being dreamlike. Diane described her feelings during the week her daughter lived:

> I kept thinking, "It's a dream. I'm going to wake up. They

drugged me!" They didn't, but I thought, "Maybe they gave me a medication for labor and I'm just dreaming." And that happened several times over that week. Or I thought, "Oh, this isn't true."

A strong sense of helplessness and lack of control was expressed. "Crazy" behavior was common. Several parents found themselves acting in ways that did not make sense, and this was frightening to them. The most common immediate emotional reaction to this perception of helplessness was depression and aimlessness. A small number of parents responded with frustration and anger. For others, anger became a more common emotion only after time progressed.

In every case and regardless of the type of loss, the parents reported an initial sense of shock and disbelief. They could recount small pieces of their experience in great detail, describing the clothes they were wearing, the physician's manner in informing the parents of their child's death, even the content of entire conversations. But these were often fragmented and isolated remembrances. For the most part, they could remember only bits and pieces, details were fuzzy, and they spoke of "moving in a fog" or "just going through the motions." Ross's 9-month-old daughter died suddenly. For him the time after the funeral was

like a blank. . . . You're not thinking real clear. Nothing makes sense and you really don't care what happens next. The worst has already happened.

At the time of their loss, parents attempted to defend themselves against the assault on their original structure of meaning. Before the death, they may have been able to deny the seriousness of the situation, refusing to believe the news that their child was in danger or, particularly in pregnancy loss, that their baby had actually died. Although effective as a short-term coping strategy, these efforts ultimately were inadequate to allow them to maintain their assumptive world. Compounding this, strong pressure exists for persons who have experienced a loss to define the event and to integrate the new information related to the loss with their existing assumptive world in order to establish consistency between old and new schemata (Horowitz, 1976, 1979, 1986). As a result of these pressures, each respondent began to incorporate long-term coping responses in the often slow process of coping with the impact of the loss on their assumptive world.

COPING: RECONSTRUCTING THE ASSUMPTIVE WORLD

With the death of their child, these parents faced a meaningless world in which they felt helpless and out of control (Marris, 1975). After the initial disorienting impact of the event, they attempted to cope with their loss by doing one or more of the following: establishing a sense of structure in their lives in order to regain a sense of order and predictability; gathering information about the experience of others; searching for meaning in their experience to regain a sense of purpose; blunting information that was too painful to deal with at the time; and sealing over those aspects of their experience that, after consideration, they realized could not be integrated into their assumptive world.

Establishing a Structure

After their initial confusion, our respondents focused upon establishing a day-to-day, or even hour-to-hour structure in their lives. Through careful, conscious structuring of their daily activities, they developed a baseline sense of order from which they were able to operate. With a more immediate focus, activities were directed at establishing a daily routine. These short-term strategies served a dual purpose in that they also allowed parents to distract themselves from the pain of loss, a process to be described in greater detail later in this chapter. Indeed, many parents spoke primarily of their efforts at establishing a structure as a way to distract themselves from "thinking about the baby and crying all the time."

Parents expressed a strong desire to "get back to normal" or to return to a "normal rhythm." Long periods of unstructured time were difficult to tolerate and a particular problem for those who were not employed or who, as in the case of one man, a fireman, had long unstructured periods as a part of their occupation. Going to work was sometimes helpful because it routinized at least part of the day. It was not, however, a panacea, as some of the women worked in situations that required them to see small children or pregnant women on a regular basis. For them, work acted as more of a stressor than a help in finding structure.

Regularly scheduled activities took on special significance as points of focus in their routine. For many, church attendance became important, not only because of the religious significance, but because it was something to look forward to each week. Another source of structure for one-third of these individuals was attendance at support group meetings. In some cases, regularly scheduled visits to the grave were incorporated into normal family activities.

A highly methodical approach to reestablishing structure was common. Organizing their days, planning family outings, and arranging times to "have fun together" were conscientiously plotted out. Miriam described her efforts to return to a normal sleep pattern following her son's death. A disrupted sleep pattern was a common occurrence for others in this situation also.

I had to get into a system of going to bed directly at 11 and I'd get up exactly at 7, even if I was tired because, other than that, I couldn't sleep.

Another method of structuring that was mentioned by four of the women was keeping a diary or writing a chronology of their experience. As Terri said,

I put a lot of my thoughts down and it'd been so crazy that
it felt good to sit down and write down what I had been
feeling . . . to put things down in some kind of order.

A few individuals were eventually able to schedule a time to
think about their baby. Although mechanical at first, this
became easier with time.

At first, when Timmy first passed away, we didn't really
get to pick and choose, pick and choose when we were
gonna think about it. But now, when I think about it, you
know, it's a time when I'm feeling OK, when I'm feeling
positive, and I try to keep it positive and think of the positive sides of what he would've meant to me and been all
these kinds of things. [Spencer]

Gathering Information

In addition to immediate concerns about reestablishing order,
efforts were made to gather information about the experience
of pregnancy loss or infant death. Parents attempted to determine their own position on a continuum of the healing process.
Comparisons with others who had also lost children were
extremely common; each person had done this at some point.
This helped them to establish a sense of their own recovery.
     Conversations with fellow survivors of child loss as well as
attendance at bereaved-parent support groups were helpful in
constructing this feeling of recovery. In a similar way, the ability
to look back and see that a pattern existed in their behavior and
that they were moving toward recovery also gave a sense of
order.
     Setting goals, both short-term and long-term, provided a
sense of direction. Goals could be as apparently simple as walking through the baby section of a department store or attending
a family function where there would be children. A very com-

mon long-term goal was having another child, either by birth or through adoption.

Search for Meaning

In addition to establishing some new sense of order, parents begin early in their bereavement to search for meaning in their tragedy (Hamburg, 1974). During the process of resolving their grief, respondents reported asking themselves and others a number of questions. As previously discussed, Figley (1983, 1985) has suggested that answering these questions allows parents to master their loss experience cognitively and establish a coherent sense of meaning. Questions triggered other questions as they went about the business of constructing a healing theory.

Hamburg and Adams (1967) have suggested that seeking and utilizing information are useful strategies in coping with traumatic events. Accurate information was cited as essential to their recovery by these men and women. Through reading and conversations with medical professionals and others who have gone through a similar experience, they gathered information about various aspects of their loss. Medical information was solicited about the cause of death. The cause frequently was unknown or based on symptoms rather than the causal agent or agents. The inability of the physician to explain such factors in a satisfactory way was very difficult to accept. This was especially true for those persons who wished to have other children. The urge to find a medical cause was so strong that if one could not be determined or the one they were given did not satisfy them, parents deduced a cause from available information.

Information about responsibility or fault on the part of medical professionals frequently was sought. In addition, parents also tried to determine the extent of their own responsibility. They wished to know if there was a physical cause to which they contributed and if it was correctable. They also needed to come to terms with any possible error in judgment on their own part.

> It's very important . . . after the death to find out what happened . . . whether it be, like there might be something wrong with the mom or dad. [Roger]

> I guess I wanted to . . . know all of the why for her [the child] and why for me, why, what was wrong with her and what was, you know, why did I deliver, that kind of thing. And kind of knowing the facts seemed to help, for some reason. [Monica]

Along with medical information, being told what to expect in the grief process was helpful. A majority of these individuals had never experienced such a loss and did not know what to expect. In order to increase their knowledge base, they sought out other survivors of child loss or attended parent support groups.

Although it is believed that trauma victims need to ventilate their feelings and get support for their ideas (Janoff-Bulman, Madden, & Timko, 1983), for these bereaved parents, the need to talk with others varied greatly. A few individuals said they felt a strong need to talk at first, with the urge diminishing over time. A small number of individuals, primarily men, stated that they preferred to listen to others, gaining comfort from this. Commonly, individuals who chose not to talk either found their emotions burdensome to discuss or found strong emotions intimidating and painful. A larger group found it not only helpful but essential to talk about their baby.

> I did a lot of talking about the baby where, after the baby died, after she had been born, you feel an almost incessant need to talk about the baby to make it real. She had dark hair and her eyes were sealed up, she had a little mouth, that kind of thing. . . . I talked incessantly. You're very

proud of that baby. It's your baby. The fact that the baby
didn't live doesn't change that fact. [Kay]

For this group, talking about the baby validated the existence
of that child, something those who had experienced a loss of
a fetus or a newborn felt a particular need to do. Speaking of
their child gave substance to mental images. In a sense, it
seemed necessary to give substance to their hopes and dreams
for their wished-for child before they could abandon these
dreams. Talking about the death itself also made it less
dreamlike and more of a reality.

Talking with others was found to be helpful to respondents
as they developed their healing theory—that is, their explanation for what had happened, why it had happened, and what
might go on if it happened again (Figley, 1983, 1985). By discussing elements of their theory, they were "validating their
reality," as Berger and Kellner (1964) have termed it. For a
majority of these individuals, this became problematic as more
and more members of their support network tried to get them
to "forget it and move on, get on with your life," or refused to
discuss the baby at all.

Twenty-four individuals attended a support group at least one
time. Of this number, seven couples attended together over a
period of time, two couples went one time, and six wives
attended alone. This gave these parents an opportunity to
express their emotions and explore their growing healing theory
in a supportive and understanding environment. Other ways
in which support groups helped in the development of a healing
theory included the availability of a lending library and guest
speakers at group meetings who presented information on
what to expect in the course of grieving.

Support groups also served as a source of other parents who
had lost children, with whom these men and women could
compare themselves to determine how they were doing in their
own grieving. Such comparison was a common strategy. Those
who had no context within which to determine healthy and
unhealthy behavior—that is, what was "crazy" and what was

not—created such a context by determining what others had done. In addition, those who had experienced other losses also compared their present experience with those they had had in the past. As has been discussed before, this gives a sense of progress in grief resolution.

Positive and negative comparisons provided an opportunity for these parents to gain perspective on their loss. "It would have been worse if . . ." was a common way of comparing themselves with some self-constructed worse scenario. Examples of this very common means of coping include the following:

> [My mother's friend's] baby . . . was strangled with the cord. Now something like that . . . that would be much more of a serious loss to me than at the 13-week period where I didn't feel any . . . movement. [Karen]

> I think that would be much worse to lose a child that you had around the house and that you were accustomed to. And this, although at the time, you think that this is the worst thing in the whole world. But looking back now, you realize that would be worse. [Lynne]

> It'd be even harder, to me, to get to know a person, get more attached . . . think maybe [of] these parents whose children are older. It, you know, may be even harder than it was on us. [Charlie]

Religious beliefs and faith in God were questioned by several respondents in relation to the baby's death. Almost half of these individuals specifically stated a belief that "there's a reason for everything" even if they were not privy to that reason. Prayer and a belief in a kind and loving God were helpful. The image of their child in heaven also brought comfort. Rita, a teacher of handicapped children, knew that her daughter would have faced a life of pain, had she lived. Her strong belief in a kind and loving God made the acceptance of her daughter's death easier.

In some ways, it's much easier for me to think of her in heaven, not hurting. [Rita]

Jonathan also spoke of the loss of his daughter and his pain in not being able to share "all the beautiful things in life" with her. He went on to say,

She can see it all the time now, you know, the beautiful things. . . . She's in a better place now than she ever would've been here, but we still would've liked to have had her here. [Jonathan]

A strong belief in a just and controlling God prevented a small number of men and women from finding their religion to be helpful for a time. For these individuals, their belief in a just God who rewarded good and punished bad caused them to question their own "goodness." If they were to retain such a belief, the child's death might have been seen as a result of their own flaws. At the same time, the belief in an all-controlling God led them to blame God for their loss. In order to reconcile their experience with their religious beliefs, several of these persons reshaped their beliefs in God and came to see that their loss "was not of God" and that their religious faith could help them to deal with their thoughts and emotions afterward. None abandoned their religious beliefs as a result of their loss. This topic is examined more fully in Gilbert (1992).

A special concern of over half of the parents was that the child should be memorialized in some way. Activities directly related to their child's death, such as the funeral and visiting the grave, particularly on holidays, were common. Several individuals made contributions to medical research. Others saved mementoes, such as pictures, birth certificates, toys, and materials from the hospital. Others wrote down their feelings about the baby or wrote poetry. Special ornaments were hung on the tree at Christmas time; arts and crafts, such as picture collages and needlework, were displayed. For Linda, who had experienced two separate early fetal deaths at approximately 13 weeks into

each pregnancy, symbols were the only way that she was able
to establish any sense of reality for her lost babies:

> and there was this [a charm] that I had on when I was
> pregnant. I made that into a family symbol. It was two
> doves with a heart between them and a little heart hang-
> ing. . . . It's hard not to think of the two babies now . . .
> it's a reminder.

Another means parents chose to memorialize their child was
through helping others. Parents volunteered at such places as
local schools, the town library, and nursing homes. On other
occasions, they helped other bereaved parents to deal with their
loss. In addition to serving as a memorial for their child, these
activities allowed them to focus on something other than their
own situation and often gave them a sense of purpose and perspective. This form of coping also may have served as a key to
how far they had come in their own grieving.

> Maybe the turning point is when you can talk to other peo-
> ple or call up somebody who's lost a baby and say, "What
> can I do to help you?" 'Cause, otherwise . . . you couldn't
> talk about it, face it yourself. [Jennifer]

The search for understanding is often slow and arduous.
Regardless of their efforts, these parents may find it impossible
to answer all of their questions. The process is often painful
and, at times, the search for meaning may seem fruitless. In this
case, rather than continuing to attempt to process information,
they used other, avoidant forms of coping.

Blunting

At different times in the parents' grief resolution process, the
pain of dealing with the reality of their baby's death and what
the loss meant to them was too great. At such times, informa-

tion was blunted. As Miller (1979) has suggested, blunting strategies serve to remove the individual psychologically from a threatening situation. However, rather than completely disso-ciate, individuals selectively blunted only those elements of their loss experience that were too painful for them to face at that specific time.

Blunting is the basic form of coping used during the time around the endangerment and death of the baby. For some per-sons, blunting strategies, as well as sealing over (to be dis-cussed next) dominated throughout the grief process. Others used a more balanced combination of all five forms of coping.

During the period leading up to the child's death, the seri-ousness of the situation was often denied. Some parents pro-crastinated about responding to symptoms or insisted that some error had been made. At the time of their child's death, five of these men and women chose not to see their newly deliv-ered child. Others chose not to view their child's body at the funeral. As they attempted to return to a normal rhythm, cop-ing strategies described above under "Establishing a Structure" were used to distract as well as structure. Indeed, such behav-iors often served both purposes, allowing the individuals a period of emotional safety as they reorganized the structure of their daily lives.

Sealing Over

It is difficult, if not impossible, to construct a completely sat-isfactory healing theory. For some participants in this study, their assumptive world and certain aspects of the baby's death could not be fitted together. These participants had some ques-tions that they came to accept as unanswerable but that contin-ued to cause, at the minimum, occasional sadness or pain. When these unanswerable questions were "sealed over," certain aspects of the event could exist "immune from the demands of having to be integrated with the view of self and world, prior to the event" (Smith, 1981, p. 42), thus allowing them to function otherwise normally. Sealing over legitimized the reality that some or all of the event could not be integrated into the assumptive world. Later, this sealed-over portion of the event could be "unsealed" and incorporated into the healing theory. It may also be possible that the event would remain sealed outside of the assumptive world permanently.

> . . . just the fact it's so unexplained why she died. Can't explain it, why it happened. There just is no answer. . . . It's an explanation that there's no explanation. We'll never be able to understand in our lifetime, at all, why such an adorable little girl should die. [Ross]

Grief may be sealed over when it is felt that there is nothing for parents to do to come to terms with their child's death. In fact, for some individuals, the process of "working through grief" or dwelling on an event that generates intense emotion is alien to them.

> I have a tendency to not dwell on things I can't change or prevent. [Wayne]

> I accepted it . . . it's over . . . that's the way it is. Life goes on. [Roger]

Eventually, most parents sought to leave their pain behind. Rita recounted her decision to stop questioning their daughter's death and to begin the process of moving on.

> I said, "I'm just so tired of hurting, I want to stop." I don't want to forget Cheryl, I just want to stop hurting.

It did not seem essential that the healing theory, developed to explain the loss, completely incorporate their baby's death into their assumptive world. It may have been enough that they were able to understand some of their loss while they sealed over the rest.

RECURRENT GRIEF: BREAKING
THROUGH THE SEAL

Until traumatic events are integrated into the assumptive world, intrusive images of the event will recur (Horowitz, 1976, 1979, 1986; Figley, 1983, 1985). In the case of the death of a child, this sometimes involves painful memories of the loss experience. Because parents expected and planned for their children to survive them, they "grow old with grief" and are never able to leave it behind (Rando, 1984). In a study of parents who had experienced a perinatal loss, Rosenblatt and Burns (1986) found that almost 25% of parents who had lost a child during pregnancy or early infancy experienced occasional or frequent pangs of grief. Some of these pangs were described as intense, even though the time since death ranged from 2 to 46 years. Peppers and Knapp (1980b) also observed what they referred to as shadow grief among women who had experienced fetal or infant loss. This phenomenon of recurrent grief was also found among a majority of respondents in our study. Only two said they had never had such an experience.

In general, episodes of shadow grief lessened in frequency and intensity with time; there were, however, exceptions. A small number of individuals who primarily had blunted and sealed over thoughts of their experience to cope with their loss experienced sporadic episodes of intense recurrent grief, often accompanied by rage or symptoms of depression. Henry spoke of his efforts to contain his grief and his resultant anger outburst:

> You want to cry and you can't do that so you stretch it out and then, there comes a time, at 6 months, I figure, when a man just goes nuts. You just hold off everything. Then all of a sudden, something triggers it . . . you go off. You go berserk.

Situations that elicited a similar emotional response often

acted as triggers. Usually the following pregnancy was extremely stressful, with significant points in the pregnancy and delivery acting as triggers. Threats to another child in the family, such as major surgery, could cause a recurrence of thoughts of the baby they had lost. Rachel had spoken of "putting the whole grieving process on hold" when she became pregnant subsequent to her son Andrew's late fetal death. Later, another son had surgery from which he almost died. In discussing her unusually strong reaction, she said:

> I found myself thinking, you know, more about Andrew and talking about him more. . . . There wasn't the numbness there was to the original degree, and so . . . the second crisis . . . brought back the feelings and they were much harder because there was not the additional numbness and disbelief that accompanied it the first time around.

The ability to identify what acted to trigger episodes of recurrent grief varied greatly. Some persons were unable to identify any triggers; others could provide highly detailed lists. The range of triggers was extensive. They included significant dates (e.g., the anniversary of the death, the due date for pregnancy losses and preterm births); general times of the year (e.g., springtime, the holidays); visual cues (e.g., seeing other babies or children); auditory cues (e.g., hearing a baby cry); and olfactory cues (e.g., the smell of a particular flower, the smell of Pampers diapers). If named, triggers often had highly specific meaning for the individual.

> I remember seeing my little nephew and his red hair and thinking our baby was probably going to have red hair. I just always thought that. . . . And seeing him laugh and smiling and realizing our baby wasn't going to do that. [Linda]

> At church, there's four sets of twins. And every time I see

them walking down, dressed just alike, "Oh, I could have had one of them just like that!" And one of them is even Donna's age. And they're little girls, both of them and her same build and tiny. And it just reminds me, over and over again, that we could've had two. [Dolores]

As they worked to resolve their grief, the bereaved parents in our study used different combinations of coping strategies. Eventually, the cumulative effect was one of moving the individual toward a new sense of meaning and a reconstruction of the assumptive world.

REORGANIZATION: A NEW CONTINUITY OF MEANING

The resolution of grief takes place over the course of the grieving process. It is a highly complicated, idiosyncratic process, dependent on the individual's pattern of organizing meaning, the assumptions held by that person, the extent of impact on those assumptions, and the coping strategies used to deal with those impacts. The death of a child disrupts the assumptive world, and the recovery from grief depends on regaining a sense of continuity of meaning in the assumptive world, one that incorporates the death of the child. As assumptions are questioned and new ones constructed, the developing healing theory functions as the bridge between the old and new assumptive worlds.

Grief resolution is highly individual, progressing at rates that vary greatly from person to person. Some of these individuals came to terms with their baby's death very quickly while others found it necessary to work through the process in slow and halting steps.

Sort of like when you break your leg. It isn't after awhile you just walk. You walk a little every day. You just heal. That's it. You just heal. [Henry]

As they worked to resolve their grief, these parents placed their child in perspective. They came to realize their child would not grow up and would not have a future with them. Writing about divorce, Waller (1967) noted that part of the assimilation of experience is that there is a "dissipation of affect" (p. 283). Feelings become less intense; grief and love lose their charge, but do not cease entirely. "A large part of the solution of many emotional problems consists in the admission that they are likely to remain always with us and in developing a technique for living with them painlessly" (Waller, 1967, p. 285).

> I feel like that it's a part of me and really, I want it to stay a part of me. I don't think it really belongs to anyone else. [Ken]

> I think Cheryl is in the perspective of my life. She's in a good place. She's important but she's in the past. And I don't know how to say this, she's a part of my daily life but she's not a part of my daily life. She's not here. Her needs are fulfilled. . . . I know how I feel about her and that's never going to change. I'm always going to love her. [Rita]

Initially, several individuals went through a period of isolation, either self-imposed or imposed by others. As they moved toward the reorganization of their assumptive world, they were able to feel a part of the world again. They began to entertain and accept invitations. They also began to learn to enjoy themselves without their earlier feelings of guilt.

In addition to their specific questions about their loss, other areas of their lives came under scrutiny. Several respondents questioned their values following the death of their child. In their interviews, they spoke of how they had come to a new assessment of the importance of career and family and their desire to have a child. For many, a new and sadder realism was described that included the fact that babies die and death is a part of life.

CONCLUSION

As these bereaved parents have shown, grief is a "redefinition of normal." It has an effect that is sometimes dramatic and devastating on the assumptive world, a set of beliefs that are used to organize perceived reality. In order to come to terms with this disruption of the assumptive world, the parents must regain a sense of structure and gather information about the loss in order to develop an understanding and create meaning for their loss. At the same time, such efforts often increase stress, leading parents to blunt those aspects of their loss that are too painful to face or seal over those parts of the loss that cannot fit into their assumptive world.

As they move toward reorganization of the assumptive world, bereaved parents often experience periods of recurrent grief. In the following chapters, we explore the ways in which couples dealt with each other in their efforts to cope with different and sometimes conflicting patterns of grief. In Chapter 4, we will show that the patterns of initial and recurrent grief episodes experienced by spouses were often out of synch or incongruent with each other, thus leading to conflict and dissatisfaction between partners. Chapter 5 concentrates on positive means of coping in the dyad during the grief resolution process.

4

The Couple and Grieving

Destabilization

The shared loss creates a new and very profound tie between [bereaved parents] at the same time the individual loss that each of them feels creates an estrangement in the relationship. (Klass, 1988, p. 42)

The death of a child creates a paradoxical bond (Klass, 1988) between parents who simultaneously share a loss and yet may sense that their experience of the loss is different from their partner's. Some of the parents in our study emphasized the shared bond between themselves; others talked almost simultaneously of the comfort and pain of knowing that their spouse also was grieving.

For all of these couples, the loss created at least a temporary destabilization of the relationship. For most of them, the destabilization became a crisis, in that the marital system's customary coping mechanisms were not adequate to meet the demands of the situation. The death of a child affects parents as individuals, as we saw in the previous chapter. Parental bereavement is a unique stressor in that it affects both spouses directly, both spouses indirectly (as each spouse must deal with the other's reactions to the death), and the marital relationship.

Each marriage consists of two individuals, and yet paradoxically there is a third entity present, the relationship. There is, from the perspective of each partner, an "I," a "you" and an "us." What each spouse perceives, wants, or needs may differ from what the other spouse does, but the relationship part, the "us," also has needs. For example, "I" may want time alone to relax, "you" might want "me" to spend time with the children, and "our relationship" might need "us" to spend the evening talking and making love. The three entities that make up a marriage may not always agree even in the best of times. When a major stressor event, such as the death of a child, hits the relationship, satisfying all parts of the marriage becomes even more difficult.

This chapter and the following chapter examine the process involved in interactive dyadic bereavement. We examine how the couple deals with each partner's own emotional response to the death while simultaneously dealing with the demands of the relationship. In this chapter, factors that contribute to the destabilization of the marital relationship—that is, result in marital strain—are explored. The following chapter will address factors that lead to restabilization of the marital relationship—that is, reduce or prevent strain.

Resolving the death of a child, when examined in the context of the couple, is a complex process requiring continual adjustment of each partner's coping in relation to the other's. This process requires the integration of each individual's experiences, perceptions, feelings, and reactions to the loss and follows different patterns, over different periods of time, to different degrees for both partners.

As indicated in the previous chapter, the resolution process is not consistent and linear for each person. Several different processes occur simultaneously, as parents attempt to come to grips with the death of their child. Intense emotions are experienced as the reality of a future without their child is faced, accepted, and integrated into their assumptive world. The symbolic meaning of the loss may be different for each parent, and the resulting emotional reactions to the loss may be quite disparate. At any given time, each spouse is likely to experience the loss somewhat differently. The interactions of these different processes and related conflicts come together in the marital dyad.

DYADIC BEREAVEMENT AND MARITAL STRAIN

As defined by Boss (1987), strain is a relational variable, "a mismatch between the accumulated demands made on the [couple] and the resources to meet these pressures" (p. 701). Following the death of their child, the spouses are placed in a position of needing to cope with their own felt stress resulting from the loss while also attempting to cope with its impact on their marriage. Thus, dyadic coping consists of efforts to reduce the stress on the individual while also minimizing strain on the bonds of the marital relationship.

For these couples, the primary source of marital strain was a mismatch in the way in which spouses interpreted one another's behavior, conflict over both partners' view of themselves in relation to their spouse, the way both viewed the other acting in relation to themselves, and expectations of the marital relationship itself. The ultimate result of the mismatch was marital disharmony, which destabilized the marital relationship and increased the stress on individual partners.

DESTABILIZATION OF THE MARITAL RELATIONSHIP

At one time or another in their grieving process, almost every couple in this study experienced some level of relational strain or estrangement, which contributed to the destabilization of the marital relationship. Only one couple could be described as having a total absence of marital disharmony during their grief resolution.* The remaining 26 couples were distributed along a continuum from those experiencing little disharmony to those having episodes of extreme, relationship-threatening conflict. For the most part, couples fell into the middle of the range in terms of levels of conflict reported. In general, it appeared that

---

*The only couple who did not experience conflict was unusual in many ways. Both partners held similar beliefs and values along with a uniquely positive way of looking at life.

marital conflict was episodic in nature and largely resulted from an underlying disagreement in beliefs and expectations.

Conflicts over Beliefs and Expectations

As indicated in the previous chapter, parents experience a strong need to attribute meaning to the event in order to integrate it with their assumptive world. By interacting with others, parents legitimize for themselves the new meanings that they create (Berger & Luckman, 1966). Spouses have special power to validate or invalidate the beliefs and perceptions of each other, and their doing one or the other assists or impedes the realignment of their assumptive worlds (Berger & Kellner, 1964). Spouses are able to consider and confirm each other's view of what has happened, is happening, and will happen. As they work to make sense of their loss, spouses compare and attempt to gain confirmation from each other of their beliefs, opinions, hunches, and private theories. Affirmation of one's expectations, including expectations for the other spouse's behavior, contributes to a sense that stability and control have returned, facilitates communication, and provides structure and meaning to interactions between spouses. When spouses did not affirm each other's expectations, they felt less stability and control, and were less satisfied with their communication.

As has been suggested by other authors (Borg & Lasker, 1989; Peppers & Knapp, 1980b), a common problem for many couples in this study was that one or both partners expected that the other would have a similar, possibly identical, grief experience. This problem was particularly evident when one or both partners were in the midst of an intense grief episode with a related reduction in their own coping abilities. Factors were present that prevented a common grief experience from taking place. They included differences in the following areas: the meaning that each parent gave to the loss; the view that each partner held of themselves as a couple; their views of appropriate grief behavior; and their individual experiences surrounding the loss.

THE MEANING OF THE LOSS

Although both parents experienced the same objective loss—both lost a baby in infancy or pregnancy—there was usually a disparity in what the loss meant to each of them. Rando (1984) and Arnold and Gemma (1983) have suggested that each parent experiences a different symbolic loss and that it is this symbolic loss with which they must cope. This was certainly shown to be true for these parents.

The most clear-cut examples of this were the cases in which the baby died during pregnancy or near birth. Klauss and Kennel (1976) found that the mother usually develops a stronger attachment and a greater sense of "personhood" for the baby at this time because she has carried the child and observed changes in her body. Evidence from these couples was consistent with these findings, as the greatest disparity between husband and wife in attachment to the baby was found with the couples who went through a very early pregnancy loss, that is, before the mother's body began to show obvious signs of pregnancy. In both cases in which this occurred, the mother experienced the death of what she perceived to be a baby. The men, on the other hand, responded very differently from their wives:

My emotional attachment was such that I was disappointed. Of course, I had only recently decided that I thought I really wanted to have a child. . . . I guess I sort of felt, in a way, it's too bad and I hurt and I felt, personally, that we need to go on and see what the doctor says and try again. [Phillip]

After it was over, I think my strongest reaction actually was one of relief. In a way, I was kind of relieved that she wasn't pregnant, that we were not going to have a kid. . . . It was, like, breathing space. . . . It was harder on Karen than it was on me. . . . [For me it] was . . . almost a trial run. [Roy]

In addition to there being incongruent bonding, spouses found they did not share the same imagined future for their child. In this, mothers appeared to think about and plan for a child earlier than the fathers did, regardless of the stage of the pregnancy or the age of the infant. As a result, the experience of being pregnant and giving birth to a baby seemed to have more meaning for the mothers and, consequently, often led to a·stronger reaction on their part. Because of this and other factors, marital partners were surprised, even shocked, to find a disparity in what each spouse had to resolve in the grieving process. Gail spoke of the differences between herself and her husband following their daughter's preterm birth and neonatal death at approximately 23 weeks' gestation.

> I had dreamed about her room, that she'd grow up to be a Democrat. I tried to get [my husband] to talk about what his hopes and dreams had been for her. He didn't plan, at least as far in advance as I had for her.

THE VIEW OF THEMSELVES AS A COUPLE

The couples in this study often described their marriage as a good one prior to the death of their child, a source of comfort and pleasure. In fact, one striking and possibly anomalous characteristic of these couples was their strong sense of marital commitment, to their partner and to marriage as an institution.

In depicting their marriage prior to the loss, these couples spoke of a relationship in which they saw themselves as sharing common interests, goals, and values. They described a marriage in which they had established a system of dealing with normal day-to-day life where each of them fulfilled prescribed role behavior, including supporting and comforting the other. The death of their child and their own as well as their spouse's reactions caused them to question assumptions about their marriage, their spouse, and themselves in relation to their spouses. As Rita said in describing her actions following her daughter's death three hours after her birth,

Goodness, I'm not a selfish person. I never have been, but I really was during this. I just hurt so bad and it mattered to me that he was hurting and I remember thinking about it, but I just couldn't see. Nothing mattered enough to me to act on it. You know, I remember thinking, "Poor Gordon," but that's as far as I got. I'm ashamed of it but it's true. I really can't think of anything I did to help him.

Thus, at the same time that these spouses found themselves overburdened by their efforts to cope with their own situation they were attempting to provide comfort, support, and a willing ear to the other spouse. The result was a perception of distance in the relationship.

EXPECTATIONS OF APPROPRIATE GRIEVING

As was discussed in Chapter 3, each individual implemented certain behaviors to cope with the loss, which were combined in a unique and idiosyncratic approach toward coping with grief. Frequently, this led to a high degree of disparity between spouses in their grief and coping. In addition, partners brought different ideas with them about the best way to respond to the loss. The end result often was a clash over how they should act.

Husbands and wives spoke of how they could not agree on the way to regain a sense of stability and meaning in life. A complication of this was that the meaning of the loss changed over time for each partner. New information about the cause of death or exposure to a triggering agent might cause a recurrence of shadow grief for one spouse, accompanied by an increase of grieving behavior. Such a change in behavior could be seen as frustrating and counterproductive on the part of the other. They also disagreed about what to do with the emotions generated in the process. In general, men tended to find emotions unproductive while women tended to believe that the expression of emotions was essential to recovery.

Marital partners also found themselves trying to influence or control one another's behavior. Advice on the need to "move on," to "stop feeling sorry for yourself," or to "stop avoiding your feelings" fell into this category. These efforts generally were made to get the other to grieve in what the adviser believed to be the correct way, sometimes to help the partner to give up and move past the grief and, in other cases, because one partner thought the other was avoiding or denying grief. This was most troublesome when couples took highly disparate approaches to grieving or were at different points in their grief resolution.

THEIR INDIVIDUAL EXPERIENCE

As Lindemann (1944) said, grief involves work, and this "grief work" is exhausting. Fatigue is common among the bereaved and, indeed, the parents in this study spoke of debilitating exhaustion. Again, even though both mothers and fathers reported this, they often named different causes.

In instances in which the child died in pregnancy or near birth, the mother had to cope with the physical loss of the child and related changes to her body. These changes fatigued her and added to her physical pain because they served as a constant reminder that her baby was now dead.

I remember the hard part was trying to get my milk to dry up and how . . . I didn't realize how painful . . . it was more painful just because of memories that it brought. [Monica]

In 12 cases, the delivery was complicated and the mother's recovery was slow. During their convalescence, these women were alone with their thoughts for long stretches of time. Women who were not employed outside the home and did not have the distraction of work also found their emotional recovery to be slow, at least in part because of their sense of isolation.

When there were medical complications, husbands initially faced a situation in which their wife's health, perhaps her life, was threatened. Each man had to deal with his reaction to the death of his child and the threat to his wife. They described feeling helpless and out of control and the sense of loss at being unable to talk to their wives about their feelings. At the same time, social support from outside the marriage was directed toward the wife while the husband was expected to be "the strong one" for the sake of his wife, the person who was perceived by others as the one who had experienced a loss.

> All the requirements were being given to Kay. She was the one who was in danger of dying and was the one who was losing the baby. And one of the unfortunate things was that the father, throughout the entire situation, gets, "Well, it's tough, buck up buddy." But nobody cares about the father. [Henry]

Men spoke of the stress of maintaining the family, facing financial worries, needing to go to work and being expected "to produce one hundred percent." At the same time, they felt the pressure of serving as the principal or only support for their wives. The intensity of the situation increased with time, as people outside the marriage became less and less sympathetic to expressions of grief. A stressor commonly noted by men was their feeling of complete isolation in their efforts to cope with their own grief while supporting their wives in theirs.

Finally, for all the parents, there was some highly specific aspect of the loss that contributed to the feeling of estrangement. They were reluctant to share information about this with their spouse, to some degree because of a belief that their spouse could not understand what they had gone through. Another motivation for this reluctance was to protect the spouse from further stress.

As with other aspects of the loss, the subjective interpretation of these experiences was what made them uniquely upsetting; the same experience that distressed one parent would not necessarily bother another. Examples include one parent's seeing and holding the child after death while the spouse was unable or unwilling to come into the room, or one parent's going alone to the mortuary to select the baby's coffin. In one case, the father delivered his stillborn son by the side of the road while traffic sped by. In another case, the mother was holding her daughter in her arms when the baby suddenly had a seizure and died. Thus, each parent dealt with memories that were singularly distinctive to him or her.

Disparate experiences with death and other losses prior to the death of their baby along with different expectations about grieving resulted in dissimilar behavior on the part of each parent, and for many couples, this contributed to the perception of their grieving as incongruent.

CONFLICTS OVER GRIEVING

Incongruent Grieving

As has been suggested by others (cf. Miles, 1984; Peppers & Knapp, 1980b), conflict between husband and wife comes primarily from disagreements about their methods of grieving. This appeared to be the case for these couples. Lisa found coping with the contrast in their grieving was the hardest aspect of her interactions with her husband.

[You] experience your grief in different ways, at different times. Incongruent grieving, isn't that what they call it? And you know, you almost want to go through everything together. . . . You feel like you're not [and] it's just terrible.

A perception of incongruence can occur at any point in the grieving process. This perception was related to expectations about how one's spouse should have been acting. As Lisa's statement indicates, the most common form of incongruent grieving found in this study was based on the expectation that both parents, having experienced the same loss, would also experience the same grief and engage in the same mourning behavior. This is a common problem for couples who have lost a child (Miles,

1984; Peppers & Knapp, 1980b; Rando, 1984). In a less frequently seen form of incongruent grieving, one partner
expected the other partner to grieve differently, because their
loss experiences had been different. Following the neonatal
death of their son, Melissa found her husband Nick's insistence
that they were experiencing the same grief to be unacceptable.
She said,

> . . . I don't think he understands that. Whenever I'd say
> this is bothering me or dealing with my moods, he'd
> always say to me, "I don't think you realize it's just as hard
> for me as it is for you." And there never was any recog-
> nition that maybe there was a little more I was going
> through.

The interpretation of the behavior of one's spouse rather than
the behavior itself was the basis for perceived incongruence. For
many of these couples, observable differences in grief behavior
existed from the point at which they began to grieve. Most commonly, one partner described himself or herself as numb or
stunned while observing the other partner being able to weep
or "grieve openly." Usually, however, this was not seen as negative, but simply as a part of the other partner's immediate
response to the situation. For the most part, partners did not
begin to identify negative differences in their spouse's grief until
after the initial period of confusion and disorientation described
in the previous chapter. Later, when they began their efforts to
regain a sense of continuity in structure and meaning, inconsistencies in grief behavior became noticeable and irritating.

THE MOST APPROPRIATE CHOICE OF GRIEF AND COPING BEHAVIOR

The most common form of conflict over grief resolution was
related to what each partner perceived as the appropriate choice
of behavior. Each person coped with grief in a unique and idiosyncratic way, based on individual perceptions and needs and
on the person's view of what was appropriate behavior for a

man or woman. These differences commonly led to disagreements between spouses over the appropriateness of each other's behavior. Generally, one spouse found one form of coping to be helpful while the other spouse responded in a very different way.

> I remember how Wayne and I could read the same book and we would both see different things in it. One, in particular, comes to mind. Wayne keyed into several passages that said parents should resume normal activities as soon as possible. I found several that said that people should be allowed to grieve at their own pace. I remember arguing about his need for me to return to "normal" sooner than I was ready. [Gail]

Conflict often resulted when one person preferred to deal with grief in private while the other wished to talk and to share feelings. The most common pattern was for men to prefer to "work through" their grief without discussing it. In some cases, one parent thought it inappropriate to communicate information about his or her emotions. In others, the emotions generated by discussing events related to the baby and the death were too overwhelming to address. As is shown in the following examples, this form of coping was more common among men.

> I'm the one who don't talk much. I keep it inside. She's just the opposite. She needs to talk to somebody and that's what made it pretty hard for us. . . . I was feeling pretty bad about the situation. I could not talk about it. Couldn't. [Peter]

> I could never, probably, show my grief. I could never tell myself, "It's OK." I never did . . . I only cried a couple of times. [Patrick]

Another situation that resulted in dyadic disharmony occurred when one person found it necessary to leave the home and stay away for a few hours at a time. This contributed to a sense of isolation and rejection on the part of the spouse. Most of the time, the person doing the leaving was the husband. Other couples described a situation in which the husband, exhausted and depressed, would come home from work and, although physically present, would mentally isolate himself.

> I was a zombie and I parked myself in front of the TV. . . . "Just leave me alone, I'm trying to survive this!" [Alex]

THE MEANING OF BEHAVIOR

Each spouse operated from his or her own frame of reference, identifying certain behaviors as productive in grief resolution. When the other spouse chose behaviors that were different or contradictory, these behaviors were seen as unproductive. The inability of one spouse to interpret the other's behavior as healthy and appropriate to the situation, along with the related sense of unpredictability, was highly stressful. At the same time, the person whose behavior was being evaluated felt angry, isolated, and frustrated at the lack of sensitivity on the spouse's part.

> We had spats during this time. . . . It was usually over my coldness to the situation. . . . She felt that I . . . didn't act concerned or something when I really was concerned. [Ken]

> We've had some good arguments, fights, when I've been down and everything else . . . and, of course, it's all because of keeping things inside for a long time about Eric. It's like you don't care, you don't talk about him. He says, "I care but I just keep it inside." [Cassie]

MOURNING BEHAVIOR

Couples also disagreed about appropriate mourning, the public display of grieving. Most commonly, one spouse felt that the other was engaging in some public display of emotion that was not seemly, such as openly weeping or involving others in continued discussion of the baby. (Usually, but not always, the offending party was the wife.) In other cases, the wife was offended because the husband wanted to participate in highly visible activities, such as participating in a parade or running for public office, shortly after the child's death. The wives viewed these activities as inappropriate because, as they expressed it, "We were supposed to be in mourning."

Because of their sense of combativeness over these behaviors, agreement could not be reached on attending public functions or entertaining during the first year after the death. Holiday gatherings were particularly trying during this time. As was the case with private behavior, the different meanings that these gatherings held for each spouse were the source of the disagreements. For Wayne and Gail, the Christmas after their daughter died was especially troublesome. Wayne tried to talk Gail into attending family gatherings with the thought that this could serve as a distraction from her intense grief. As he said,

> I tried to encourage her to get out and not spend so much time dwelling on the problem . . . to see her family, see my family. She wasn't willing to do those things.

For Gail and Wayne, these parties meant something completely different; for Gail, they could not serve as a distraction as they did for her husband. For her, these get-togethers were a constant reminder of her daughter's death, only months before.

> We had Thanksgiving and Christmas to go through and I had all of these dreams about being nice and pregnant for the holidays with the families and all that. . . . I didn't want to be around children.

PATTERN OF GRIEF RESOLUTION

In addition to conflicts over specific grief behaviors, 10 couples reported arguments over the pattern through which they moved to resolve their grief. As Bowlby (1980) suggested, if there is a great disparity in grief resolution, stress is placed on the marital relationship. Patrick and Faye, whose son had died four years prior to the interview, had to deal with the realization that they had been resolving their grief at very different rates. At the time of the interview, Faye believed she had worked through her grief to the extent that she had "sorted out my feelings," was satisfied with the way in which she had come to terms with the death of her son, and only sporadically experienced grief pangs over his death. Her husband's grief was quite different.

> I'm lingering it out. She had it all first and then is tapering off. I'm just spreading it out for an infinite number of years . . . [Patrick]

> It's like he's in slow motion through all the processes. . . . That's why it's been hard. [Faye]

Disagreements also arose when one spouse had reached a point in the process of resolving grief where he or she felt the time for emotion had passed and it was no longer productive to "dwell on the past." At this time, these spouses found themselves less sympathetic to their partner's need to talk and process emotions. Ken talked about a point, several months after his son's death, when he found it difficult to talk with his wife about her continuing, active grief:

> It was hard on me cause I felt like, you know, she was dragging it on and on and I'm trying to put it behind me but she kept wanting to put it back in front of me again. See? And I didn't know what to do.

SETTING FAMILY GOALS

As a result of their differences in grief and coping, one partner, usually the husband, began to plan for the future sooner than the other did. Arguments resulted when that person pushed to set family goals before the other person felt ready. This was especially true when the goal was having another child. If this was mentioned as a conflict, it was usually the wife who was opposed to attempting another pregnancy. Most often, this was due to a fear of losing another child. Even if this fear was not rational, it still affected her. As Dolores said,

Stan wants more children and I don't . . . ,you know, I don't want to go through that again.

Interestingly, once the decision was made and a pregnancy was initiated, the husband sometimes would begin to express fear and apprehension about the outcome. This difference between spouses may have been the result of differences in readiness to begin to plan compounded by a tendency on the part of the men to minimize the risks while the women tended to maximize the risks. Later, faced with a pregnant wife, the men were unable to deny the seriousness of the situation.

Other Sources of Conflict in Grieving

COMPETITION IN GRIEVING

Occasionally, the awareness of incongruent grieving escalated into a type of competition over whose grief was worse. This competition could involve both partners' attempting to prove that they had suffered more than the other. At other times, one spouse perceived their experiences to be identical because they had both lost the same child, while the other spouse saw his or her own situation as worse. In the latter case, women cited their physical loss as well as their emotional loss; men spoke of their lack of support and the feeling that they had to cope in isolation.

RESONATING GRIEF

Another problematic form of grief occurred as a result of marital partners grieving in close proximity to one another. Cornwell et al. (1977) described this type of grief, in which husbands and wives would influence each other's emotional state. Most frequently, one spouse would begin to weep and the other would then do the same. Jane described a more extreme version of this resonating grief:

> I could go to work and I might feel pretty good at work and I might come home in a good mood. Well, he'd been home all day with nothing but thoughts. And I might come home and he might have tears running down his face and say, "I need a hug." And I would resent the fact. "I feel good! Why are you pulling me down?"

BLAME

Although it was expected that some partners would blame each other for the death, only one woman spoke of her anger with her husband for their baby's stillbirth. In this case, the husband had medical knowledge and by denying the seriousness of her symptoms may have contributed to the death of the baby and her serious medical complications following the birth. In all other cases, respondents seemed particularly sensitive to the need to avoid blaming each other and often spoke of how destructive this sort of blame could be.

Interestingly, a sort of "nonblame" argument took place in some cases. In this situation, one parent, usually the mother, would claim that she was somehow responsible for the baby's death. She and her husband would then argue over her guilt or lack thereof. Wayne described his frustration at not being able to convince his wife, Gail, of the irrationality of her self-blame.

> She always blamed herself for the loss of the child, which I could never get her away from to this day. . . . She'd make comments about it wasn't fair, that she was being punished, that she was a bad person, that it was all her fault, that she should have known that she was going through labor earlier. . . . Well, I try to comfort her and it becomes frustrating because there wasn't any helping.

CONCLUSION

Bereavement in the context of the couple involves coping not only with one's own grief but with the grief of one's spouse as well. A majority of these couples experienced some degree of marital strain and disharmony related to their grieving, largely because of the necessity to focus on themselves and their own needs or an inability to accurately interpret their spouse's needs. The end result was incongruent grieving for a majority of couples.

Although a majority of couples experienced some level of relational strain over their grieving, each couple was able to balance this strain with relationship-affirming coping strategies. In the next chapter, the ways in which couples coped to maintain or reestablish their relationship will be discussed.

5

The Couple and Grieving

Restabilization

Any couple who tells you after the baby died, they're so much closer or so much happier, is full of it. [Kay]

At the time that the child died, Dolores and I had always considered ourselves to be close, but I never spent a lot of . . . quality time discussing things with Dolores or spending a lot of time with our older son. . . . We're still getting over some of the things that were brought up between the two of us. But overall, our marriage is a lot stronger than it was before. [Stan]

In the previous chapter, we examined factors that contributed to strain in the marital relationship. The marital strain was of sufficient intensity for a third of these couples to worry about the continued existence of their marriage or "just how functional this marriage would be."

In this chapter, aspects of the dyadic grieving process that prevented or reduced marital strain are explored. How did these bereaved couples reduce the feelings of strain and enhance the stability of their marriage? By exploring the character of positive interactions described by marital partners, it is possible to draw a picture of ways in which a marriage is held stable or restabilized after a period of conflict. As has been indicated previously, the marital partners' subjective interpretation of their experience and the experience of their spouse was of central importance in their grief and coping responses.

STABILIZATION OF THE MARITAL RELATIONSHIP

With the exception of one couple, all respondent couples went through some level of relational destabilization after the death of their baby. Yet all of these couples were able to increase the sense of relational stability and lower the level of strain in their marriage. They did this through the following: the quality of their communication; the degree to which they held a positive view of themselves and their marriage; their ability to see the loss as shared; their sensitivity to each other's needs in coping with the stress of the loss; and their flexibility in their perceptions and actions toward each other.

Marital Communication

The ability to engage in open and honest communication has often been seen as essential to recovery from loss (Figley, 1983; Raphael, 1983; Rando, 1984). Supportive communication is assumed to facilitate discussion of emotions and developing healing theories of the event. Open communication increases the likelihood of understanding and acceptance in the family (Figley, 1983). As was expected, when the partners were asked about what they saw as most helpful in their relationship, the most common answers were related to communication in their marital relationship. Often, their ability to communicate with one another was seen as particularly important because these couples frequently felt ostracized by others outside the marriage. Their ability to talk with one another gave them a sense of being connected and allowed them to test and confirm their growing healing theories. Even those persons who were relatively taciturn agreed with this position. Ken, for example, found it difficult to discuss his emotions surrounding his son's death. Yet, when asked to make a recommendation to other bereaved couples, he said,

Talk it out. Just keep talking it out . . . till the issue is settled. I mean the death . . . come to an understanding with each other. If they have any problems, you know, then discuss it openly with each other.

The exchange of information increased a sense of mutuality and understanding for these couples. For the most part, when the child was ill or at the time of death, only one parent was able to act as an information gatherer and had to convey this information to the spouse. Possibly because so many deaths were preceded by complicated deliveries, husbands most frequently acted as the information gatherers. The ability to convey accurate information was useful in answering questions that the couples might have had about the death and each other. Later, as they attempted to make sense of the death, the ability to discuss their evolving theories about what had happened was a valuable coping tool.

Discussing any future they had planned or visualized for their child was helpful in understanding and accepting differences. For those couples who had highly disparate images of their child's future, this was often a revealing experience.

EXPRESSING EMOTIONS

As suggested by Helmrath and Steinitz (1978), the ability to cry together and display deep emotions in each other's company was frequently seen as helpful. The strong emotions generated by the loss were sometimes surprising. Seeing someone else as apparently distressed as oneself validated these emotions. Lisa found her view of her loss validated by her husband Roger when he wept openly for their daughter: "Seeing his pain . . . showed me he cared."

Openly expressing their own emotions was particularly difficult for approximately half of the marital partners. Listening to the other spouse express emotions was sometimes beneficial for these individuals. Those who finally were able to reveal emotions to their spouse found it to be a positive experience for themselves and their marital relationship.

He never used to express his feelings so, and for him to cry in front of me was very traumatic for him. And when it turned out it was no big deal, he realized it takes a real man to cry and get their emotions out and really talk things out. [Willa]

Support groups are often seen as valuable information sources (Edelstein, 1984). Only seven couples attended a series of support group meetings together. For two of these couples who found it difficult outside of the group to share their feelings with each other, attending a support group became a "safe haven" for expressing their emotions to each other.

It was mainly within the context of the meetings. It was like, you know, that was where we had permission to do it. So we did it there and maybe a little bit in the car on the way home. [Rachel]

We talked about it for a while after the meeting, then things started building up and we wouldn't talk and we'd go to the next SHARE meeting and it was like we could talk about it again. . . . If we hadn't had something like that to go to, I don't know what would have happened 'cause we would have just gone on. [Rose]

LISTENING

A common theme running through interviews was the need for one or both partners to have the other spouse listen. Women, in particular, found that their need to talk about the baby was almost compulsive. A willing ear on the part of the husband was especially appreciated. This need was often exacerbated by the sense of isolation and stigmatization generated by the unwillingness of others outside the marriage to allow them to talk about their child.

Listening to the spouse expressing emotions contributed to the stress of the listener, especially if the result was conflicting feelings on the listener's part. Even though this resulted in increased personal stress, these listeners persisted because, in their view, they were helping their spouse to come to terms with the loss. Indeed, their willingness to listen was viewed by the person expressing the thoughts and emotions as very meaningful because it validated the legitimacy of his or her feelings and the acceptance of their differences. This acceptance can be extremely important when the partners form different attachments to the child and experience very different emotions at the death of the child. It can also facilitate the resolution of conflicts in expectations held by the two partners.

NONVERBAL COMMUNICATION

Spouses found it difficult, at times, to speak to one another of their thoughts or emotions. At these times, nonverbal means of communicating were used instead of or in addition to verbal means. This use of nonverbal communication was especially common among persons who dealt with their emotions in a more private way. Individuals spoke of communicating with their spouse using "body language" or having a "comfortable understanding." In some cases, they could not identify what it was that let them know that their spouse's emotional state had changed; they simply sensed this change.

> His mood would just change and then I would be the one to say, "Yeah, I saw those little girls over there. They do look alike. That could have been us." [Rita]

CODE WORDS AND SIGNALS

Another means of communication was a system of verbal and nonverbal shorthand that allowed partners to communicate with one another without letting others know. These private systems of communication allowed them to exchange a great deal of information, using single words or phrases. For Cassie, a sense of awareness on the part of her husband was a part of their normal relationship.

> He knows when I turn quiet, something is bothering me. And I think a lot of the time now, he doesn't really probe why I'm quiet. I think he just, after so many years, he knows. And a lot of times, I'll say, you know, "I need a hug."

A Positive View

One of the most distinctive characteristics of couples who reported very little conflict was the positive view they held of each other and their relationship. Indeed, one key to whether or not they were still actively grieving was if they could find something positive in their experience or in each other. This ability to key in on the positive may be another characteristic of many of these couples that makes their grief experience unusual. As indicated in the previous chapter, they did not blame each other and, in fact, emphasized the importance of avoiding a negative outlook on each other. These individuals spoke of their spouse as "the best thing that ever happened to me" or "the most important person to me." In addition, many couples took an optimistic view of life, looking for "the good things in life. The bad will always be there. Let the good ones shine."

For six couples, it was necessary for one or both partners to "bottom out" before they were able to begin to look for anything positive in life. The deteriorating health of one partner or a threat to the marriage served as this turning point in three cases. In the most extreme case, 18 months after the death of her daughter, Tamara developed cancer and was forced to examine her attitude toward life:

> I realized that I had to change my attitude towards life, that I had to forgive Ross and praise God that we were all

still alive, that there were still years ahead of us all. There would be happy years ahead of us all.

The remaining couples began the shift to a more positive view slowly. At first, only certain aspects of their relationship were framed in a positive light and, from that point, they continued to expand their positive view. For example, spouses were identified as "my best friend." The appraisal that they were lucky to have each other was quite common. The image of themselves as a couple who needed each other was also solidified through the grieving process. In this regard, at least one partner in 24 of the couples indicated that the experience of dealing effectively with the death had a positive effect on their marriage. For 18 couples, both partners said the experience had a positive effect on their marriage. Couples learned they could survive such an event and, in many cases, become closer and more tolerant of each other.

I think I really feel that even though this is something we experienced that . . . I think it made us more aware of what I had to be thankful [for] rather than dwelling on the loss. [Susan]

REFRAMING

A coping skill found to be extremely useful in the move toward a positive view of each other was reframing (Nichols, 1984). It involves changing the conceptual or emotional viewpoint of family members in order to change the meaning of their behavior without changing the actual behaviors themselves (Watzlawick, Weakland, & Fisch, 1974). By positively reframing their spouse's behavior, individual partners altered their perception of their spouse's behavior. In some cases, this took place after they had tried to influence their spouse to change the behavior. This appeared to be a natural process for these individuals, and the urge to put their spouse's behavior in a positive frame was quite strong. Indeed, during the interview, when asked about what their spouse did that was not helpful, respondents often answered and then, immediately afterward, gave an explanation of the behavior that put it in a more positive light as the following examples illustrate.

For Lisa and Roger, the significance of receiving public support at their church resulted in a bitter argument. He argued that their loss was not something that should be discussed by others; she felt the opposite. At the same time, she felt tremendous pain and anger because she felt this meant that her husband's faith was not as strong as hers.

> We came home in silence and I cried as hard as I ever cried . . . it was horrible. Now I can say we experienced our grief at different times.

Karen and Roy experienced very different emotional reactions to the death of their baby early in pregnancy. This difference was quite painful to accept at first. Now Karen is able to say,

> It really made us a lot closer. . . . It showed that we deal with things very differently but that we could talk to each other about it.

The first few months after their daughter died, Fred and Jane could not seem to get "in synch" in their grieving. Whenever he was up, she was down, and vice versa. After beginning to attend a parent support group, they learned that this was normal, and now Fred can say,

> If one of us is having a good day, you know, the other would seem to be in the pits . . . and I could just look at her, tell by the way she looked that she needed a hug. . . . One of us needed to talk, you know. And whatever the one who was down wanted to talk about, that was fine.

In addition to being used by one spouse to create a more positive image of the other spouse, reframing was used to seal over information about the other spouse or the relationship that con-flicted with expectations that had existed prior to the loss. In doing this, reframers allowed themselves to accept that their spouse had some characteristics that did not fit into their orig-inal assumptive world regarding that person. As Gail said of her lack of agreement with her husband, Wayne,

> I'd say that, other than Marcie, things are pretty much the same. We've always had a very open, warm marriage. He's my best friend and I'm his and I like that. It's just the one area.

By putting a positive frame on their disagreement, and essentially agreeing to disagree, Gail could then move past their serious disagreements about the loss and continue to build a relationship with her husband that allowed them to continue to be close as a couple. At the same time, it allowed her to move away from disagreement about whether or not they should view their daughter's death in the same way.

Sharing the Loss

The ability to develop a shared view is considered important to resolution of stress in the family (Reiss, 1981) and particu-larly important for traumatic stress (Figley, 1989). When these couples were able to see the loss as one that they shared, not necessarily as the same experience but one in which they felt they were available to each other, they felt a greater sense of con-nection between themselves.

> There's another human being there sharing this with you. I suppose the idea is it's being shared. It helps. I guess that would be the main strength that she was able to give me was that there's someone here that loves me and also loved Timmy, and I love her and vice versa. [Spencer]

Couples spoke of "being there" for each other or "having each other to lean on." In this capacity, partners helped one another to answer their questions about the death and get on with their lives. They were also helped themselves because, as we saw in Chapter 3, the partners' ability to help another person was seen as a positive method of coping with grief as well as an indicator that they had reached a point in grieving where they were able to focus on something other than their own loss.

GRIEVING TOGETHER

Couples who grieved together were physically available to each other, hugging and touching and occasionally talking. Jonathan and Diane felt they were particularly lucky in that they were able to stay together at the hospital after their daughter was born. They believed that this set the tone for the way in which they dealt with their grief, which was essentially conflict-free. As Jonathan said,

That was the saving grace as far as we were to help each other, that we were together, that she would wake up in the middle of the night and reach for my arm and we would, maybe, talk for a minute.

Grieving together did not mean that these couples were at an identical point in their grief resolution, but that they spent a great deal of time in each other's company. By being together, they were exposed to more information about each other's grief. This increased the likelihood that they would accurately interpret each other's behavior.

EXCLUSIVITY

Spending time with each other, without any other obligations, was found to be very helpful, especially in the days or weeks immediately following or surrounding the death. Five couples used a vacation to escape the demands of others and the immediate triggers of memories of their loss. In order to guard their privacy, couples did such things as turn off the telephone for a period of time, refuse support from family members, and isolate themselves until they felt that they could both face outsiders without being upset. Two-thirds of the couples had older children in the home, and caring for them was sometimes exhausting, partly because their questions were difficult to answer. For these parents, time alone together, usually for a few hours while a relative or friend watched the children, was helpful because, "a couple needs that time to themselves."

It is important to be aware that these couples did not find an extended period of isolation to be helpful. They did feel that their time alone as a couple established the loss as their own. Their identity as a couple who had experienced a loss together was important to both of them.

SHARED FOCUS

Having something to focus on outside their marital relationship allowed couples to work as a team, to concentrate on something other than themselves, and to emphasize their identity as a couple. Because so many of the couples (18) already had children at the time of their loss, children most frequently served as the focal point. This shared focus on children was described as very helpful to both partners in coping with their grief.

Working together to help other bereaved parents was another point of mutual focus. Acting together to aid other family members to deal with their reaction to the death, although frustrating at the time, was also seen as having a positive effect on their marriage. In both of these cases, such mutual focus served to distract spouses from their own grief, allowed them an opportunity to increase communication, and gave them a point of comparison to assess their own and their partner's grief resolution.

In addition to working as a team to solve some problem outside the dyad, couples also built a shared focus within their marriage. Common were shared rituals, such as regularly visiting the grave, which legitimized their connection to the child.

For half of the couples, the immediate shared focus was on the health of the wife. In one case, the husband was seriously ill at the time of their son's death and both the husband and wife turned their attention to his needs. Although for most couples, this focus was very short-lived, in two cases, it continued to serve as a shared focus at the time of the interview. In one of these cases, the wife had been hospitalized for an extended period after the delivery and continued to experience complications at the time of the interview, four years after the death. In the other case, the focus had initially been on the wife's emotional health. Six months later, when she developed cancer, the focus shifted to her physical health.

COMMON GOALS/COMMON VALUES

Another way couples found to pull together as a unit was by directing their efforts toward some common end. Often, this allowed them to regain a sense of themselves as a couple.

> You gotta have something to look forward to together. Nothing unites like common enemies, common goals. Gotta find an enemy or a goal. [Ross]

Ironically, the effort to identify a common goal was also seen as a source of conflict, if one party identified the goal before the other was ready. Only when both parties felt that they had contributed to the selection of a goal and that they were ready to carry it out did it act to reduce strain on the relationship.

In addition, common values, especially religious values, were important. This need for a common faith may be due to the fact that religious beliefs serve as the basis for much of the assumptive world. The beliefs themselves were not as critical for the marital relationship as was the commonality of these beliefs. Thus, consistency between partners' beliefs about the religious meaning of the loss were more important than the form these beliefs took as far as marital strain was concerned.

Another common value seen in these couples was the importance of marriage, both marriage as an institution and marriage as a relationship with this individual. In each couple, at least one person stated a belief in the importance of marriage.

Flexibility

For the couples in this study, flexibility was the ability to change as the need arose or to accept some type of information that contradicted previously held beliefs. This information could come from observation of or interaction with each other.

ACCEPTANCE OF DIFFERENCES

Initially, most couples found accepting the existence of differences in their grief to be a problem. Incongruent grieving was common as couples attempted to cope with their own loss experience. As couples became aware of the bases for these differences, though, they became more tolerant of one another.

> I think you have to realize that you are two different people and you grieve differently and to allow each other the personal privacy. [Kay]

For those cases where conflict was low, this realization came very early in the grieving process. Jonathan and Diane saw that even though their grief experience was shared, it was necessary to grieve separately, too. As Jonathan stated,

> We had to deal with it ourselves, between us. [Diane being] . . . supportive was fine but I still had to deal with it myself at some time.

When partners experienced different emotions over the loss,

they found it helpful to have the belief that "it was OK for me to feel the way I felt" acknowledged by their spouse. This reduced the strain between them and allowed each to stop feeling guilty over not grieving in the "appropriate" way. Although experiencing incongruent emotions was a problem for many couples, this was a particularly significant issue for those who had experienced an early fetal death.

The term "space" was used by two couples in describing the ways in which they respected one another's individuality. Gordon and Rita accepted this sentiment when they said,

> I tried to give him the space that he gave me. . . . I tried to allow him to grieve however it happened to work best for him. [Rita]

> We respect each other's . . . space. . . . I've got to have my private time and then [at] the same time, she's got to have hers. [Gordon]

ROLE FLEXIBILITY

If one spouse was incapacitated and unable to respond normally, the other spouse would step in. Often, this role trading or sharing centered around routinized tasks that were a part of the family routine; for example, child care, household tasks, running errands. In many cases, this easy shift of role performance within the family was mentioned as having been a normal part of their relationship prior to their child's death.

For one couple, this flexibility took the form of a complete role reversal when the husband, stricken with a serious illness immediately prior to his son's death, was hospitalized, and the wife had to take over his responsibilities.

> As far as Maeve and I were concerned, it was a complete role change because now she had to get better, not necessarily for the baby's sake, but for my sake. [Will]

More usually, husbands took over their wife's household responsibilities without being asked. They cooked, did the laundry, and took care of older children.

> Nick would go to the store for me, and he would take the kids when he needed to go and that kind of thing. He was doing the ironing. [Melissa]

Sensitivity to Each Other's Needs

Another way in which partners attempted to reduce marital strain was by watching their spouse and responding to what they perceived to be the needs of their spouse. This was successful when the spouse receiving the support confirmed that it was helpful.

> We both tried to work together a little bit more than normal. I tried to watch closely and pay attention to her feelings more. Probably more in tune with that, to how she was feeling . . . more so than normal. [Charlie]

Almost half of the participants spoke of "little things" that their spouses did that made them feel important. This might be as seemingly simple as a man bringing a potted plant to his wife so that she would have something to carry on her way out of the hospital. In one case, the husband took time off from his job, without pay, to be with his wife. Another husband decided that he had "a mission" to help his wife through her grief. Two women mentioned that their husbands had purchased items of jewelry that had great symbolic meaning, a mother's ring in one case and a commemorative charm in another. These items validated their emotional connection with their baby. A woman's efforts to meet her husband's needs might have involved attending carefully to his emotional state so that she could determine his ability to talk. Women also responded to their husbands' need to regain a sense of structure and order. Their way of doing this included baking a cake that was a particular favorite of the husband's or getting back to cooking meals or organizing the household.

Sometimes these efforts to respond to the needs of the spouse were done to reduce tension in the home. Often, respondents found that helping their spouse and focusing on meeting the needs of their spouse also benefited them.

> I think she did a lot for me. . . . She had a lot of deep feelings and when I start thinking about the type of feelings she's having, that helped me to have those . . . that, maybe, enabled me to be able to cope with this thing better. [Spencer]

To some extent, providing support to the spouse served a dual purpose. Focusing on the other spouse may have been helpful because it distracted those individuals from their own pain. The "helper" spouses may also have learned ways of coping by observing the "helpee" spouse. Finally, helpers may have experienced a sense of moving toward recovery because they were able to help another person rather than needing help themselves.

Finally, in addition to being aware of their spouses' needs, participants found that by accepting their own limitations, recognizing their own needs, and not trying to be everything to their spouse, both partners benefited. Rather than exceed their abilities, they encouraged their spouse to go to appropriate resources outside the marriage. Three of these men stated a belief that their wives needed to talk to someone else and encouraged them to speak with other women or a clergy member, or attend a support group.

CONCLUSION

The grief of married individuals requires coping with not only one's own grief, but the grief of one's spouse as well. Although most of these couples experienced at least some marital strain related to their own grieving, they also were able to achieve at least some stability in their marital relationship. They did so through a variety of means, including communication (the exchange of information, the expression of emotions and thoughts, and the ability to listen to one another). A positive outlook on their relationship and the perception that they had shared their experience also was helpful. Each partner's sensitivity to recognize differences and flexibility to adapt to the other's needs also reduced marital strain.

In the next chapter, the marital relationship is examined from another perspective, that of gender roles. Many of our respondents spontaneously spoke to us about the impact that their loss of a baby had upon their feelings about themselves as men and women. Many of the individuals believed that men and women react differently to pregnancy loss and infant death, and they framed their behavior in terms of these differences.

6

The Function of Gender Roles in Dealing with Bereavement

I had always thought that males should be able to open up, but there's always been the stigma associated with males, who are supposed to be big, tough, macho guys. But we've got feelings too. And I think that the public ought to be made aware of it and allow men to express their feelings openly and not be ashamed of the fact that, "Hey, I cry!" [Fred]

And [my wife asked me], "Do you want to go to [the local support group]?" And I said, "Not really . . ." Some people like to get up and talk about it and all this. I feel like it's a part of me and I really, I want it to stay a part of me. I don't think it really belongs to anyone else. . . . I didn't want anyone interfering with my feelings. Try to tell me how to feel or tell me I wasn't feeling enough remorse . . . [Ken]

GENDER ROLE BEHAVIORS AND EXPECTATIONS

Gender role behavior consists of socially structured behavior patterns learned in the context of being a female or a male. Girls learn to act and think like girls, and boys like boys, from endless observations, and instructions, praise, criticism, glances, and hints from parents, teachers, siblings, friends, and, in fact, everybody.

The process continues throughout life, with even grandparents learning their roles as they receive information from family, friends, and the media. An important part of courtship is observing the gender role behavior of the potential spouse and discussing what he or she expects of a wife or husband. It is very unlikely, however, that in their explorations of gender roles and expectations for self and other that any couple will speculate on what they will do if they have a baby who dies.

Along with learning behavior patterns considered appropriate by the social world in which one grows up, each person also learns to evaluate behavior as being right or wrong for males and for females. Thus an individual has gender role expectations for boys, girls, men, and women. Some expectations are very specific, such as that the ushers seat the friends of the bride on the left side of the church. Other expectations have to do with personality characteristics that persist throughout life, but the expression of which is not spelled out. For example, men are expected to be tough, and women tender. It is easy to follow a clear, definite role prescription or a series of actions or rituals. It is difficult or impossible to produce feelings on demand, or to behave in ways that are not in accord with the feelings a person is experiencing.

At the death of a child or an adult, parents know what to do. Rituals such as wakes, funerals, and the Jewish custom of sitting shiva provide structure for bereaved individuals and members of their social network. In the case of pregnancy loss, there is no such structure. Even if bereaved parents manage to have a comforting ritual, they still face questions of what to do with their feelings of loss and sadness, how to relate to each other, and how to deal with the rest of the world. They may never have known anyone who lost a baby, or if they did, they probably never discussed it with them. Silence usually reigns on this topic, broken perhaps by a suggestion that it's best to forget this unfortunate incident and get on with one's life. With little or no guidance on specific behavior, the bereaved couple is likely to fall back on gender role expectations of a general, and perhaps vague, sort.

Differences Within and Between Couples

For any particular couple, gender role behaviors and expectations will fall on a continuum from traditional to flexible and expressive. Some couples, whom we will call *traditional*, expect women to be emotional and talkative and expect men to keep their feelings under control. Additionally, the husband and wife expect him to be the provider or main provider for the family and her to be the home manager, housekeeper, and primary parent. In *transitional** couples, spouses do not agree on the way that each spouse should enact emotional and/or work-related gender roles. Usually, the wife wishes the husband were more expressive emotionally and/or would condone her working outside the home. In *expressive-flexible* couples, both husband and wife can and do talk about how they feel. Both do housework and care for the children, changing roles as the situation demands. Usually both earn money.

In this last third of the 20th century, male and female gender role expectations vary widely. Scholars (e.g., Cook, 1988; Komarovsky, 1973; Scanzoni & Szinovacz, 1980) acknowledge a considerable range of both expectations and patterns of gender roles. Our particular interest is in the relationship between coping with bereavement and the male gender role pattern of low expressiveness and high protectiveness. We also want to know how the couple is affected by the fulfillment of and violation of expectations.

In the early weeks or months following a pregnancy loss or infant death, male and female roles are likely to be very differentiated. A man's sense of obligation to perform what he considers to be the male role (breadwinner and perhaps protector) is strong, although he may or may not feel confident in his ability to do so. The lapse in the woman's ability or willingness to

---

*We borrow the terms "traditional" and "transitional" from Hochschild and Machung's book *The Second Shift*, but change the focus from work roles to emotional roles within the family. The third category, therefore, is called "expressive-flexible" (rather than Hochschild's "egalitarian").

cook or perform social obligations is temporary. However, she is keenly aware that she has been deprived of the role of mother of an infant. The woman's ability to perform some of her roles is at least temporarily thwarted.

We did not specifically ask our respondents if they thought that they or their spouse behaved in gender-appropriate or inappropriate ways. Nor did we specifically question them as to how satisfied they were with their spouse's behavior. Rather, we asked them who gave them support; how their spouse was helpful and unhelpful; and how their marriage had changed. We found, however, that many people framed their responses in terms of what they considered to be gender-appropriate behaviors:

> [The] biggest thing that I remember is it was a time when you had to be responsible. You couldn't let anybody do for you what you were supposed to do. And it wasn't for me the macho image type thing. It was just that there were certain responsibilities and they had to be taken care of. [Adam]

> In my case, the male is supposed to have, you know, be a little bit of strength there, kind of keep things from totally crashing down. And, it wasn't easy, you know. . . . [Spencer]

> This crap about men not having emotions, not being able to show them, I don't believe in. [Larry]

> He hurt just as much as I did and he's not one of these men that's afraid to cry. [Cassie]

> I think men should show their feelings, you know, let it out. [Dolores]

Acceptance of Experience Related to Gender Roles

A number of men expressed the opinion that the experience of pregnancy loss and infant death is somewhat different for men and women, and that their personal acceptance of these differences was helpful to them.

> As a male, there's no way that I feel I could totally relate to what she experienced 'cause she carried the baby for nine months. A male. . . . , unless it's a seahorse, 'cause I guess he carries the baby, [could not] totally relate to the [female] experience. . . . I just wanted to be a sounding board . . . and let her let it out on me. [Spencer]

> I can distinctly remember that I needed to listen and watch her emotions . . . , because she's more emotional, the obvious characteristics of women more than men. [Adam]

> I think that Linda's closer girlfriends were more helpful sometimes than I could be because some of them could understand what she had gone through because they had one or two miscarriages and could be more empathetic. . . . It's very hard for me, being a man, to put myself in a woman's shoes who's had a miscarriage. [Phillip]

> I'm not a chauvinist at all, so I hope this doesn't come out wrong. But I think [when a baby dies] people are more concerned about the woman than the man. I think they were concerned about her but I know they were concerned about me, too. [Roger]

Women also expressed ideas about male and female differences. Some women accepted, either sooner or later, that their husbands had different feelings about the baby, or grieved differently.

> [Going to the support group] helped, especially the second meeting, when the men were there, 'cause a woman can't tell a man how he feels. [Lisa]

Like some of the men, some women believed that women are more attached to their babies because of having experienced pregnancy and because of physical reminders immediately following the birth:

I said, "You just don't care. She's my baby. I carried her."
Which was wrong, but at the time . . . So, he said, "I do
care." [Jane]

Men can't understand what it's like. I don't think that they
love their children any less but when you carry a child, you
know, and lose [it] and you've still got the milk [in your
breasts]. . . . He can't possibly understand what you feel.
[Kristina]

Melissa noted that following a premature birth, the wife's
physical appearance (no longer being pregnant) prompts people to ask about the baby. She is always in danger of being
reminded by an acquaintance about her loss, and then having
to deal with her emotions in public.

[I said to Nick], "As sexist as that may sound, it's different
for me than it is for you." And I don't think he understands that.

Some women, however, noted that men have it harder
because of social attitudes about male expression of grief.
Kristina, who on the one hand said that men couldn't understand how a woman felt, also said:

The men have it so much harder, I think. I remember people would come up to him and say, "I'm sorry to hear
about your baby. How's Kristina?" Never, "How are you?"

Although accepting that men are given less permission to grieve
publicly, some women thought that their husbands had less
need to do so.

I was probably grieving more openly than he was. I think
it's more acceptable for the woman to grieve and the man
has to hold up and take care of her, and, therefore, he
doesn't get his chance [to grieve]. I think that could have
happened in our situation. He was just the strong one, you
know. I don't think he ever really needed to grieve as much
as I did. [Lynn]

When differences in grieving existed, it was helpful to both men and women to find a reason for the differences. Gender role expectations provided meaning for many of the couples.

BEREAVED MOTHERS

Wives were likely to feel unable to fulfill their roles as women. A woman's expectations of herself as a mother surely includes being able to carry a baby to term. A miscarriage would represent a failure in gender expectations. She would also expect to take good care of the baby, family, and home, promoting health and growth. The death of her infant would then represent her failure as a mother. However, most bereaved mothers consider it all right for themselves, as women, to express their feelings about their loss.

Betrayed by Their Bodies

In the case of miscarriage or premature birth, the women worried that something was wrong with their bodies. Women with incompetent cervices felt betrayed by their bodies, and often also felt that they "should have known better" or "should have done something" to prevent the loss.

I felt totally responsible. I still feel a lot of guilt about it too. I should have known, should have done [something] . . . [Gail]

And I thought I had failed, you know, that it was my fault. I didn't know what I had done wrong. [Karen]

The failure of a woman's body to complete a wanted pregnancy assaulted her identity as a woman. Her ability to bear healthy children was placed into question by her experience. This feeling was more intensely expressed by women who had no living children, but also was expressed by mothers of living children. One woman reported that her mother had questioned the daughter's ability to bear children, because the daughter had suffered two miscarriages. Another couple, whose third baby was born with severe birth defects, hinted that their sex life was suffering because the wife could not cope with the connection in her own mind between sexual expression and having a second deformed baby.

Part of the husband's role became attempting to reassure his wife that they would succeed in the future.

> [Adam would] put his arm around me and say, "It's all right, we might have another one. It's OK to cry, OK to feel hurt . . ." [Lynn]

> We did a pretty good amount of talking about it . . . , having other children, that sort of thing. And I think she kept rekindling the hope that we would have a full family. [Jonathan]

The best reassurance, especially for women who do not have a living child, is a subsequent birth.

> I think that after having Nicole, having a healthy child who seemed . . . just fine. I think that's when I really let down a little bit and thought, "Well, I'm OK." [Monica]

Inability to Perform Role of Wife

Following their confinement, the mothers were temporarily unable to fulfill their role obligations to their husbands and other children. During the immediate impact period, all parents of older children received help with the older children from relatives or friends, and most also received gifts of food. As time went on, however, some women still felt uninterested in cooking or caring for the house. Husbands of these women helped the wife by not expecting her to perform her usual roles around the house for a while:

> He took me out to dinner an awful lot for the 3½ months [that the baby lived but was critically ill], knowing that I just didn't feel like cooking. [Kelly]

> He took a week off work without pay, which we couldn't afford, but he did it. He cooked for me, which he doesn't do. He does not cook. He did laundry. Anything that I needed him to do, he tried to anticipate and he did it. I tried to do that but he did a better job than I did. [Rita]

> I think it meant a lot to her for me to be at home with her and taking the time to be here, taking care of the kids, fixing supper, doing the laundry. . . . [Ed]

Sometimes, the failure of a wife to perform her role obligations was a source of conflict.

> He'd come home [after work] and I'd just be sitting there, and he'd say, "Don't you have anything fixed [for dinner]?" And I said, "Oh, I just don't feel like it." [Miriam]

> I skipped a cocktail party. [Where Nick works], they do a lot of downtown business entertaining, and in the first couple of weeks I couldn't walk down there and make cocktail chatter. . . . I said [to Nick], "I'm going to hurt you more than help you if I go down there right now. You're going to be pretty embarrassed if I get in the middle of this cocktail party with all these wives of presidents and vice presidents and break into tears." And I don't think he appreciated that. [Melissa]

Some women found another role for themselves, that of helping the bereft father to express his emotions.

Supporting Fathers' Emotional Expression

Several of the wives took it upon themselves to help their husbands to express their emotions. Melissa noted that several weeks after their baby's premature birth and death, her husband would stop crying and start yelling.

> So we came back [from the cemetery] and Nick just absolutely blew his stack because his pants weren't hemmed. . . . Instead of sitting down and saying, "I'm sorry, I felt like crying," or something, he was just blowing on all these ridiculous things, nothing things, and he did that for about three [or] four days. He'd just come home and scream—I'd come home and cry and feel better—but he couldn't quite do that any more, so he'd just explode on every other subject, and I just had to say to him, "I know what's bothering you, and the cabinet doors are not bothering you. Why don't we talk about it?" I said, "Sit down and cry, go for a run, do something, but don't scream at us."

Cassie played an active role in getting Richard to express his feelings:

> At times I could sense when he was bottling things up, and I would say, "OK, let's go to the cemetery," and that seemed to bring things out if we were at the cemetery. . . . I needed to have tears come out, plus I knew it would bring out tears for him and he would feel much better afterwards.

Spencer and Kristina both noted that Kristina had helped him to experience and express his feelings, both in general and for their baby.

> I didn't come from a background where showing emotions

and feelings was as great as [in] her background and that helped me a lot, you know. [Spencer]

These women played a traditional role in helping their "emotionally constipated" (Farrell, 1975) husbands to express their emotions.

In summary, the woman's role as mother of an infant is cut off by her pregnancy loss or the death of her infant. Because it is her body that carries the baby, she is vulnerable to feelings that she has failed biologically, especially in the case of miscarriage or incompetent cervix. Among these women, feelings of guilt or self-blame occurred in spite of the absence of blaming by the husband. The woman in this situation also is at least temporarily unable to fulfill some of her other role obligations as a wife, such as housekeeper.

BEREAVED FATHERS

Role Ambiguity

Following any parental bereavement, the father's role is ambiguous, to the point of his being placed in two different double binds (Cook, 1988). First, he is expected to be strong and protective of his wife, but he is not given any support for his own grief. Second, he is expected to grieve in a way consistent with "good grief work" (Kübler-Ross, 1981), which involves crying and the expression of sadness, which for many men is humiliating (David & Brannon, 1976).

In the case of pregnancy loss or neonatal death, however, there is even more ambiguity, because the death may be socially defined as a loss only for the mother. The mother *is* affected more directly than the father, if only because it is her body that expels the baby and that then must return to a prepregnancy state. (The *meaning* that the loss has, however, may be more salient for the father, if, for example, the father wanted the baby and the mother did not.)

Focus on the Wife

In the period surrounding the baby's birth, the father's focus may shift to the recovery of his wife. As noted previously, a number of our female respondents suffered from physical complications surrounding the birth. The husbands of these women commented that they were more immediately concerned about their wives than about grieving for their babies. In other cases, the men focused on the emotional state of their wives, rather than the physical.

> He was really a lot stronger than I was. . . . I think he was more concerned about me than the loss of the child at that time 'cause I was just so devastated. [Tamara]

The husband often is called upon to make decisions, be rational, and have things under control. For example, he may need to decide whether or not he and his wife view the baby and how to dispose of its remains.

> And I needed to make those decisions pretty snappy . . . and not be hesitant or ask her if that was her desire because of [the] mental stress that she [was] under; maybe she didn't want to make all those decisions. [Adam]

In part because others expect him to "be strong for his wife," the husband regards his behavior as responsible and necessary; the wife may regard his rationality as cold and unfeeling.

> Ross is always more practical and scientific. He's a professor, and I needed the love and the emotional kind of support, and I think I got more of that from my mom and my sister than I did from Ross at that time. [Tamara]

> I think I've only seen him cry, what, about three times, the whole time. It really surprised me when he said that he

still cries. . . . He'd let me pour my heart out, but he didn't reciprocate, and I wish he had because I resented it along the way. There were times, especially during the first year, I got mad. It was the biggest thing between us [that] he wasn't sharing what grief he had. [Faye]

Sometimes I would say to him, "You don't care; you don't talk about him anymore." [Cassie]

Some wives came to the realization that their husbands had grieved, or were still grieving, but that the men grieved differently:

[I should have understood] that he probably felt as badly if not more than I did, but he expresses it differently than I do. . . . [Susan]

Men as Avoiders

Although some women spoke about the value of going back to work as a distraction, men were more likely than women to use avoidance as a coping mechanism. Part of the reason for this, no doubt, is that they *had to* work to support the family. However, they also were more likely to use social situations as a distraction.

Well, at times I have chosen not to think about things, and the way I chose not to think about them is to become involved in something that takes up all my time so I don't have to think about it. [Wayne]

I had a bad habit of leaving and staying away for periods of time and doing nothing. I mean, just going out and talking to friends and spending time away from home. [Stan]

Previous writers on parental bereavement have noted the dangers inherent for the couples (Peppers & Knapp, 1980b) when men do not weep, openly grieve, or overtly communicate their feelings to their wives. In our study, all of the men who were expressive were appreciated by their wives for being so, and all but one of the wives of unexpressive husbands said that they wished their husbands had been more open in their expression of feelings. Cook (1988), however, maintains that fathers are unfairly expected to behave like mothers when mourning the death of a child, and that men have different, not inferior, methods of coping with grief. Distracting oneself from grief is one such coping strategy, according to Cook.

Anger

Although some mothers in this study were angry, this emotion was more characteristic of the men. About a third of the male respondents described their own anger or (in a few cases) were described by their wives as having been angry. Two of the fathers described wanting to kill somebody, in one case a doctor, and in the other, a neighbor who had nothing at all to do with the baby's death.

> You want to cry and you can't do that so you stretch it out, and then there comes a time, at six months, I figure, when a man just goes nuts and you hold off everything. Then all of a sudden something triggers it . . . You go off, you go berserk. I mean, really! It's the craziest thing. And the neighbor starts yelling and you get an axe and you want to go after the neighbor and you want to kill him. Or if you don't want to kill him, you want to hurt him very badly [laughs]. [Henry]

Another father described himself as more aggressive following what he felt to be the wrongful death of his son.

> If I'm not in a good mood, somebody might cross me, not my family or somebody like that, I might just be a little bit more testy than I would have been. . . . I've had something unfair happen to me, you know. It's you just don't

want to take it any more. This time, pow! Instead of being helpless, I'm gonna be unhelpless . . . [Spencer]

Faye described a bereaved couple that she talked to as a peer counselor:

And the couple I worked with, the husband wouldn't let her [pour out her feelings]. He got mad at her and would yell at her on top of everything else. Which was part of his way of handling grief, but it's wrong, too.

For parents who believe that their child died wrongfully, rage at the agent of death is an understandable and expected emotion (Klass, 1988). Some of our respondents believed that medical negligence was involved in the death of their baby, and these parents were understandably angrier than parents who did not so believe. Fathers were more likely to discuss their own anger with us than were mothers. When one spouse mentioned the anger of the other spouse, it was the wife who talked about the husband's anger. Thus, among our respondents, anger was more characteristic of men than of women. This difference is in accordance with cultural gender role expectations.

Role Performance

The successful fulfillment of their own gender role expectations provided bereaved parents with a sense of comfort, however small, in the face of their difficulties. Adam placed great importance on his behaving in a responsible way following the death of their baby.

It just seemed like I drew support from her simply because I knew that I was doing things for her and concentrating on her and then she was accepting [it]. That was a type of support.

Adam felt that he had done an admirable job of helping his wife, and was pleasantly surprised at how strong she was during their terrible ordeal. He derived solace by reframing the situation as one that tested them as husband and wife, and ultimately left them stronger.

On the other hand, not all men felt sure of what they were doing. Spencer, who complained of having received no social support from male friends, questioned whether he was handling the situation adequately.

> When I see a guy with a little boy, I don't go into some kind of total bereavement state or something. The thing that bothers me the most is, how should I be dealing with it now? How much feeling should I be having? . . . and I think, "Well, am I achieving my normal obligation? Am I not doing enough? Should I go over there with a pair of scissors and trim the grave every day or something?"

Still others lamented what they felt to be crushing burdens imposed by others. For several of the couples, the financial burden, actual or potential, was terrifying. Especially during the crisis period, the husbands were more keenly aware of this problem than were their wives.

> We had a problem which shouldn't have bothered us but it did bother us, probably in particular because just the old masculine thing about feeling responsibility financially as an independent contractor. . . . It became apparent that if Pam had lived, it could be as much as five or six months in the hospital. . . . We could have incurred a half-million bill and our net worth is nowhere near that . . . [Larry]

> [Finances] are one of the problems I think most men face. Because, you know, men, being the breadwinner, that's their responsibility. They can't cope with what's going on emotionally and they can't cope financially either. [Henry]

Male Support Systems

Another problem for many of the men was their feeling of isolation from support, especially from the support of other men.

I don't think anybody [gave social support]. I didn't have anybody. No males, not my father, not her father, not my brother, not her brother. There were no other males that came to me and offered me emotional support. . . . But I think that most of the guys . . . felt as though they'd be so incapable of handling the situation themselves that they feared coming to me. [Spencer]

But to be honest with you, I wish there had been a man I could talk to. Even [with] my father, I couldn't, and my dad was there all the time. [Alex]

A few of the men were fortunate to have good support systems that included men to whom they could talk. Describing his work situation as being like a big family, Roger said:

If I wanted to talk about it, we talked about it. If I didn't want to talk about it, it was business as usual . . .

[On the anniversary of Peter's birth], my father called me that evening, and he says, "Well, you know, I was thinking about you, you know, with it being Peter's birthday. . . ." [Charlie]

There were a lot of people through work and some through church who expressed what happened to them, through their miscarriages, and [they] could understand what I was feeling and some let me talk a little bit and say what I needed to say. [Phillip]

Others eventually found male support through organized parent support groups.

[At the support group] you could draw some comfort because you can talk to [another] guy who says, "Christ, I'm going broke!" You say, "I know, can't keep the bills up. What the hell's going on?" . . . At least I was able to share more of my concerns, more of my problems with other men simply because they were other men. . . . We couldn't deal with our wives because they had emotional demands that we just couldn't meet. I think it would have been easier for the women to talk and get support from other women than it was from their husbands. [Henry]

Overall, however, the men were more likely than the women to complain that social support was lacking to them, and to frame this lack in terms of gender roles. The refrain was: Men do not get support from other men. For some, this lack of support existed also in the workplace.

[Bereaved fathers] were expected to go back to work the next day. . . . They had to be back there to produce. There was no long period of convalescence for them. . . . That was tough, and I hope that [men in that situation] don't get fired. I'm sure some of them do. Some of them told their boss to go stick it. Fortunately, I was my own boss . . . [Henry]

Overburdened by Wife

A few of the men felt overwhelmed by the emotional demands made by their wives.

She's had such a hard time dealing with her own feelings and her own thoughts, and she's needed my help so much that she hasn't had a chance to think or ask me a whole lot about it. I think she has been more sensitive to me since going to these [support group] meetings. [Phillip]

Men were much more likely to express the view that grief should be set aside and the bereaved should get on with life. Following the premature birth of their daughter, Wayne's and Gail's grief reactions were incongruent and became more so over time. Wayne said that he had felt very concerned about his wife's emotional stability because she could not get her feelings under control and move on. According to Gail,

In the beginning Wayne would say something sympathetic, or maybe hold me, and then later he would say that he just couldn't understand why that was still bothering me.

Many of the men were able to temper their impatience with the understanding that women are different and feel the loss more keenly than men do. But when differences were extreme in intensity or duration, or compounded by severe financial problems, a man's emotional limits were severely tested.

In summary, the men were more likely than the women to mention feelings of anger following the death of their baby. Many of the husbands felt burdened by the multiple demands placed upon them by others. Some felt that they were doing an adequate job of supporting their wives, but that they were giving more than they received. Some complained that their wives did not understand their point of view; others said that they did not get adequate social support, especially from other men. For several men, financial burdens loomed large.

COUPLE PATTERNS

In spite of the emergence of a number of themes that relate to gender role expectations and behaviors, the overall picture is complex. Four major types emerged: traditional and satisfied, or traditional couples; traditional and dissatisfied, or transitional couples; expressive-flexible couples, in which each spouse was satisfied; and low expressive couples. There also was one couple in which the husband was more expressive than the wife.

The majority of couples had polarized grieving styles, the women being much more expressive of emotions than their husbands were. Some of these women (traditional and satisfied, or *traditional*) were satisfied with their husband's level of expressiveness. These couples accepted that men and women are different. They felt that the husband should be the strong one. These women accepted that their husbands were less expressive than they were, and they interpreted this lack of expression not as "he doesn't care" but as fulfillment of the masculine gender role.

A substantial minority of couples were *expressive-flexible*; that is, both spouses freely expressed their emotions. All of these couples were satisfied with the amount of emotional expression and social support that they received from each other. Such a wife particularly took pride in the husband's expressiveness, which she interpreted as his caring about the baby and caring for her. The husbands also felt well supported emotionally by their wives.

The largest number of the couples, however, were traditional and dissatisfied, or *transitional*. These couples displayed gender stereotyped coping styles in that the husband was rational and less talkative; the wife was talkative and emotional. The men believed that they should support their wives, and to them this meant that they should not become emotional in front of their wives. The wives, however, wished that their husbands "felt more." They thought that their husbands "didn't feel enough" because the men didn't sufficiently cry or express their feelings about the baby, or in a few instances because the husband became angry when reminded about the baby.

Lillian Rubin has written about the contradictory expectations of husbands and wives. In the early 1970s, the working-class women that she studied (Rubin, 1976) felt vaguely unhappy in their marriages, but couldn't pinpoint what the problem was. The missing ingredient, according to Rubin, was intimate communication. In a later book, Rubin (1983) details the contradictory expectations that men and women have for each other. Men, she writes, believe that they *are* expressing their feelings to their wives, but that their wives are never satisfied.

Ryder (1970) described a pattern of marital interaction in which the woman becomes increasingly emotional, and the man becomes increasingly rational. In his mind, if he is rational, she will eventually also become rational. In her mind, the only way to jar him from his rational stance is to *really* let him know how bad she feels!

Three of the couples did not fit the three patterns described above. Two of the couples were *low expressive* (both husband and wife). One of these husbands was trying hard to hold the lid on his emotions, although at times he would explode angrily. Quite uniquely, the wife wanted him to hold back his expression of grief so that he could be, in her eyes but also in his, a real man. In the second low-expressive couple, both spouses were uncomfortable with expressing their emotions to each other. The husband wished that his wife had talked more, because he thought that it would have helped her to feel better. The wife saved up her emotions during the day and cried in the shower when her husband could not see or hear her. As we noted in the previous chapter, both of these low-expressive couples found a support group to be crucial for their expression of emotions. In the third couple, the husband was more expressive than the wife. He felt more support from friends than she did, and also felt more support coming from his wife than she reported giving to him. This couple seemed less satisfied than the other "husband-expressive" couples (all of which were also "wife expressive.") They do, however, speak of an "unspoken bond" between them.

Contradictions

In this time of gender role change, inconsistency of gender role expectations and behaviors exists, both between spouses and within individual spouses (Rubin, 1983). Our respondents illustrate a number of inconsistencies.

1. *"Taking charge" as a man doesn't always mean fearing emotions.* Most men felt that they needed to take charge of the situation when their wives were incapacitated. For several of the men, the wife's crisis represented a turning point in their behavior and self-concepts, in that they became, in their words, "more take charge." Some of these men were expressive of their emotions and others were not.

2. *"Communication" doesn't always mean a great deal of verbal sharing.* Wives of unexpressive husbands more often than not wished that their husbands were more expressive of their emotions. Several of the wives in the study were also low verbal communicators, and one of the husbands thought that his wife would have done better if she had been more expressive. However, a small minority of couples could understand each other's feelings by interpreting nonverbal behaviors.

3. *Most, but not all, women value expressiveness in their husbands.* Every one of the wives of expressive husbands said that she was satisfied with his expressiveness. However, wives of nonexpressive men (the majority of men in this study) were divided in their opinions. Although more of them said they wished that their husbands were more expressive, a substantial minority accepted their husband's level of expression. And one wife seemed to fear her husband's emotional expression, noting that he had broken down only once. At that time, she felt sorry for him but felt that it was best for him to "get it out of his system."

4. *Although in general women are more emotional and expressive than their husbands, this is not always the case.* Several of the couples noted that the husband was the one more affected by the baby's death, or that he was the more emotional of the two. None of the couples who overtly described this pattern felt that it was unnatural or troublesome. In several other instances, the husband appeared to the interviewers to be more troubled than the wife by the baby's death, but seemed to be suppressing his feelings. For example, one husband's hands shook during the interview, although he said that he had resolved his grief.

CONCLUSION

Many couples who experience pregnancy loss and infant death frame their responses to the loss in terms of their gender role expectations and behaviors. Men feel the need to be instrumental and to take charge, but they may or may not be expressive of their feelings. Women feel the loss physically as well as emotionally. Husbands' and wives' grieving styles may differ, leading to misunderstanding and conflict. Spouses who are able to frame their responses in terms of acceptable gender roles find one way of achieving understanding and acceptance.

In the chapters that follow, we look beyond the couple to the responses of others. In Chapter 7, the social support received by the couple is explored. Social support can be positive (helpful) or negative (harmful) and can come from a variety of sources, including medical personnel, members of the clergy, members of the couple's religious congregation, colleagues and bosses, and friends and family members. Most of our respondents reported receiving at least some positive instrumental and expressive support from persons in their social network.

7

Sources of Social Support from Outside the Marriage

Bereaved parents face the task of mourning as individuals and as a couple, and perhaps as the parents of living children who must also be comforted. In addition, the parents are members of a community, made up of their relatives, neighbors, friends, colleagues, and acquaintances. The community plays an important role in the individual mourning process (Lindemann, 1944; Parkes, 1972). In this chapter, we describe our respondents' sources of positive and negative social support.

WHAT IS SOCIAL SUPPORT?

Social support is behavior directed toward another person, in response to the support giver's perception of the recipient's needs. The recipient may perceive the support as positive (helpful or comforting) or negative (hurtful).

Positive Social Support

According to Cobb (1982), positive social support consists of actions that make the recipient feel loved, esteemed, and mutually obligated to other network members. Positive social support provides the recipient with guidelines for behavior and an evaluation of performance. The persons who provide the support give rewards when performance meets or exceeds expectations, and either punishment or support and comfort when the recipient fails. The concept of positive social support implies that the people providing support "are sensitive to [the recipient's] personal needs, which they deem worthy of respect and satisfaction" (Caplan, 1974, p. 5). Other forms of support described by Cobb (1982) include the provision of goods and services (material or instrumental support), and interaction that facilitates the individual's development of autonomy (counseling). Research on widows and bereaved parents has found that positive social support is important for the resolution of grief (Klass, 1988). For brevity's sake, when we refer to "positive social support" we will call it "positive support."

Negative Social Support

Positive social support, however, is only one side of the picture. Several researchers (Coyne, Wortman, & Lehman, 1988; Shumaker & Brownell, 1984; Silver & Wortman, 1980) caution that persons who have experienced undesirable life events sometimes are harmed by support that apparently is intended by the donor to be helpful. This kind of support is known as "negative support."

Previous research suggests that parents who experience pregnancy loss, perinatal or neonatal death, or SIDS are likely to receive negative support rather than positive support (Cornwell et al., 1977; Grobstein, 1978; Helmrath & Steinitz, 1978; Peppers & Knapp, 1980b). Our findings, however, suggest that most bereaved parents receive a mixture of positive and negative social support. The first setting in which a bereaved parent or couple is likely to receive support (positive, negative, or mixed) is in a medical setting, when they are informed of the poor prognosis for the pregnancy or infant or when the actual loss or death is experienced.

SOCIAL SUPPORT IN THE MEDICAL SETTING

Doctors and nurses are important sources of information and are also potential sources of emotional support. Usually it is the doctor who tells the parent that the infant or fetus is dead, or that a miscarriage is about to occur or has occurred. However, nurses also communicate information to parents, even if the communicator role is officially a doctor's.

Positive Support

In general, our respondents perceived the doctors and especially the nurses who attended them to be supportive. Positive support came in the form of information, when the parents were told what had happened or what would happen, and emotional support. Information giving was perceived as emotional support as well when it was delivered in a caring, humane way.

The handling of the situation during their experience of the immediate impact of the child's death is vividly remembered by bereaved parents. The newly bereaved parents needed help in handling a strange situation. In the case of stillbirth or infant death, funeral arrangements had to be made. In most cases, the young parents did not own cemetery plots and either had to purchase them or ask a relative to donate a part of a plot big enough for a tiny casket. Some parents asked the health care providers to refer them to a funeral director. Studying cancer patients, Dunkel-Schetter (1984) found that health care providers were seen as "most effective when they provide a combination of direct assistance, advice or guidance and emotional support" (p. 89).

Several doctors communicated specific information to the parents about what to expect following the death of their infant. Larry was especially grateful to the intensive care unit (ICU) doctor who spoke with them about 15 minutes after their 2-week-old infant died:

> Dr. Smith started to counsel us and said, "Unfortunately, one of the sad parts of losing a child is it's often very detrimental to a marriage, or can be detrimental, for reasons we don't totally understand." And he said, "You will, you may have

dreams that are very frightening." And he said, "You may have a lot of doubt and self-guilt. . . . It's all very natural. We encourage you to come up here and talk to us if this occurs and you have trouble dealing with this yourself."

The doctor and the nurses on the ward had already established themselves with Larry and Monica as emotionally honest and caring. The doctor had cried with the parents when the baby's death was imminent. Three of the ICU nurses attended the baby's funeral. Monica also noted that the doctor called her to see how she and Larry were doing, although it is not clear whether he called them when the baby was in the ICU or after the baby died.

Two other couples reported that their doctors had offered specific information to them about what to expect from friends and family members or each other. A third couple was helped by the hospital social worker to prepare for the reactions of extended family members. A fourth mother reported that a member of SHARE (the Source of Helping in Airing and Resolving Experiences) had come to see her when she was still in the hospital and had warned her about the kinds of things that others would say about the death of her baby. In addition, another father said that his doctor had provided information about his son's birth defects that helped him to prepare for the baby's death. In three other cases, bereaved parents got information from medical personnel who were not directly connected to the hospital, but rather were either a friend, relative, or acquaintance. All of the parents described here emphasized that it had been helpful to learn in advance that their child would die, or about incongruent grieving or the comments that others would be likely to make.

Our respondents were sensitive to and grateful for expressions of emotions that coincided with their own feelings of grief. Doctors and nurses who wept or otherwise demonstrated their own humanness were remembered in a positive light by our respondents. Rita said that the doctor's expression of grief over her baby's premature birth was emotionally honest. Rita quoted her obstetrician as saying: "I've really gone over this in my mind and tried to think if there was something I could have done different that would have helped you [to maintain this pregnancy and avoid premature labor]."

In another case, a doctor confirmed a mother's feelings that it would be a relief to have the baby's short, painful life over with so that the mother could get on with her grieving and own life. This doctor was the mother's regular family practice doctor, not a doctor connected to the birth or short life of her baby.

As stated previously, when parents were asked who was supportive, nurses, particularly ICU nurses, were noted by a number of the parents as having been helpful. The nurses were seen as being emotionally involved with the infant on the ICU, or as fellow travelers on the journey back from bereavement. Nurses who shared their own experience with a miscarriage or stillbirth provided comfort to several of the mothers. Roy reported that the nurse who attended his wife following her miscarriage said, "I had [a miscarriage] and it was so awful," but the nurse also seemed to have recovered well. Thus, the nurse was both empathic and a role model for the wife's recovery. This combination was helpful to Roy and, in Roy's opinion, to his wife.

Negative Support

Some of the couples or individuals reported negative experiences at the hands of their doctors or nurses, although these were fewer in number than those who reported positive support from them. Hospitals or medical personnel in general were about as likely to be recalled negatively as ambivalently or positively. For example, one wife recalled the ICU nurses to be helpful but the unit itself to be cold and uncaring.

MEDICAL MALPRACTICE

Parents who believed that negligence or incompetence on the part of doctors had caused the wrongful death of their fetus or infant remained angry at the doctors or medical system in general. Two fathers in particular (interestingly, both attorneys), who had lost babies previously through their wives' condition of incompetent cervix, remained angry at doctors who had failed to give proper medical care after one very premature delivery.

> Medical treatment is bad [in this city], and I think we lost Tina because of bad advice we got right away from the beginning. We should not have had a baby right away [after the earlier miscarriage]. We should have waited, we should have gotten rid of all of the infections that are possible . . . [and] gotten in physical shape. . . . [Henry]

In another instance, the father was angry because "right-to-life" doctors in the ICU had threatened to have the state win custody of the parents' deformed infant. Frank reported that his decision to remove Connie from life support systems resulted in the baby's death only an hour before Frank was to have been served with a court summons for a custody hearing.

> And I never felt guilty. And I still don't feel guilty about what I did. In fact, I feel better now than what I would've if she'd of still been alive. Because what got me was the right-to-life people that had, that was willing to spend the money and was willing to fight me but not a one of 'em would come up to me and talk to me face-to-face. And not a one of 'em seen my daughter. And not a one of 'em would foot the bill. And not a one of 'em would come and help me take care of her. That's what got me. [Frank]

Frank also reported that the ICU nurses had poked his baby many times before finding a vein from which to draw blood:

> I got tired of watching the nurses stick pins in her and laugh, in a nonchalant way, because they did not get the vein after seven and eight tries. And I finally threw one nurse out of the room.

In a fourth case, the father was angry because their prematurely born healthy child had contracted a contagious and fatal disease while being cared for in the neonatal ICU.

> Not a couple of days before Tim died there was a little guy within just a couple of feet of us that had [the same disease Tim died from] . . . What if you've got several nurses in one of these wards, one of them might be a third as large as this room and you've got, they're just packed all in there. . . . [With the beepers and equipment making funny noises], this place is hectic and nerve-wracking. . . . Without thinking, [a nurse might change one baby and then] . . . go over and touch another [baby]. [Spencer]

Another father saw his very premature baby in the hall outside the delivery room, apparently abandoned by the doctors.

In another case, a stillbirth and subsequent serious illness in the mother was attributed to incompetent medical care provided by a small-town hospital to a near-term mother with a high fever.

> We sat in a waiting room for an hour. And all this time I had a fever of 104 and there was no triage. No nurse. Finally the girl next to me came back and told her parents that she had a pelvic infection. So there I was, 104 temperature, pregnant, and he was treating a pelvic infection. . . . Never took fetal heart tones. I asked three times! I said, "Is this baby all right?" [Terri]

CALLOUS TREATMENT

Doctors were seen as unhelpful when they caused physical or emotional pain to the mother, or gave information about the child's prognosis or death in a cold, uncaring way. One mother described her experience:

> The neonatologist was really good with [us] but the cardiologist was just, like [Miriam dusts off her hands] "Oh, ho! One down, who's next?" You know, it was just real blunt. [Miriam]

When Melissa realized that her premature baby was going to die, she began to cry. Her obstetrician said, "Now that's an appropriate response." Melissa commented to us:

I could see the textbook saying, "And upon seeing their dying child, it is an appropriate response for a parent to cry." . . . It was just blasted clinical. . . . It sort of bolted me in my tracks, and I just turned and looked at her [and said,] "What a thing to say!"

MISINFORMATION OR LACK OF INFORMATION

In a previous section, we discussed information that our respondents received from medical personnel they found to be helpful. This section deals with the negative side of information. One husband specifically stated that he and his wife had been misinformed by doctors, and that this misinformation had led to a second premature birth and neonatal death. When their first child was born very premature, the doctors informed the couple that it was a "fluke of nature." Their second child was born and died in exactly the same way.

Melanie noted that her doctor had been helpful, but that the doctor had informed them that the divorce rate for couples whose child has died is 90%! We were unable to find any studies documenting a divorce rate higher than that of the general population. However, Rando (1989) noted that Kaplan, Grobstein, and Smith's widely-quoted study (1976) of 77 parents whose children who had died from leukemia found that 93% experienced serious marital problems, including 18% who separated and 5% who divorced. We share Rando's (1989) concern that medical personnel provide accurate information to parents regarding their chances of marital failure.

Several husbands complained that hospital personnel had neglected to tell them about the availability of support groups (such as Compassionate Friends or SHARE). A number of months after their baby's death, two of these couples found out about such groups by coincidence and were helped by attending them.

> And they tried to help us at the hospital [at the time of the baby's death]. But at that time, we didn't know of any support groups and they didn't tell us about any. It was a good while afterward that we found out about Compassionate Friends. [At the hospital] they tried to tell us, "Oh, things would be all right, things would work out." But it wasn't all right. . . . It took a long time before it got better. [Henry]

In summary, immediately following the death of their infant, parents are vulnerable and in need of accurate information about what to expect. As we have explained, most of our respondents received good informational support, which is information that is accurate and delivered in a supportive way. Good informational support was perceived as emotional support by the parents. Some parents also received emotional support from medical personnel. When doctors or nurses openly grieved, genuinely expressed sorrow, or attended the baby's funeral, parents felt emotionally supported.

SOCIAL SUPPORT FROM THE CLERGY

Members of the clergy often are called upon by bereaved parents for comfort or for help in planning a burial or memorial service. At times, hospital chaplains who were previously unknown to them offered their services to the bereaved parents. When asked who had helped them, fewer than half mentioned the clergy. Six individual parents and one couple specifically mentioned that a member of the clergy had been helpful, and six individuals mentioned that a member of the clergy had been unhelpful.

Positive Support

The essence of positive support from the clergy for these bereaved parents was that the help that was provided had personal meaning to the mourners. Two parents mentioned that the member of the clergy had done an especially nice burial or memorial service. One of these ministers also did the following: visited the mother in the hospital every day, found out about burial costs, introduced the bereaved couple to two other couples who had previously lost babies, and called a year later to see how they were doing. This minister was the core of this couple's support system.

One other minister was remembered as having gone out of his way to provide solace to the grieving parents. Rita reported that her minister had stayed all night with their very premature baby until she died. This minister also visited Rita in the hospital every day.

Mentioned also as helpful were ministers who were willing to talk with parents in a comforting way. One of these ministers had also lost his firstborn. Two other parents, a mother and a father (not married to each other), said that their clergyperson was helpful, but did not specify how.

Negative Support

The essence of negative support from a member of the clergy was the inverse of positive support and left the parents feeling preached at, or feeling that the message was impersonal. Kay said that the priest who did the burial

> just came and read through some prayers. I've never seen anyone talk so fast. It was like the Federal Express commercial. Told me I should be delighted that I had an angel in heaven and then ducked. He was worse than nothing— the man was a jackass.

Several mothers felt that the clergyperson had been rude or insulting, and several additional parents said that what the member of the clergy had said to them was not comforting.

In summary, parents in our study who mentioned a priest,

minister, or pastor were about evenly divided in portraying this individual as helpful or unhelpful. Hospital chaplains, probably because they did not know the parents prior to the infant's death, were less likely to be experienced as helpful. Clergy who went out of their way to listen and comfort the parents provided solace for them.

SOCIAL SUPPORT FROM FELLOW PARISHIONERS

Members of the clergy are the most prominent representatives of organized religion to provide social support for bereaved parents. An additional source of support is the membership of the particular congregation attended by the parents. We will refer to these individuals as "fellow parishioners," although we recognize that members of some religious groups would not use this exact terminology.

Most of the couples in this study reported either being members of an organized Christian religion or attending church services, or both. Two couples specifically indicated that they were not members of a church, and three additional husbands also were not church members. Three additional couples did not clarify whether they belonged to a specific church, but they did state a religious preference.

Respondents were not asked specifically if they had received support from fellow parishioners. However, six couples or members of couples volunteered that fellow parishioners had been helpful.

Positive Support

Positive support came in the form of emotional support, including prayers, and instrumental support, including food and cash. Several couples said that members of their church had prayed for them. One of these couples also indicated that they had received word that parishioners at a church to which they had belonged in another state also had prayed for them. This couple also said that since their baby's death, they had become more active in their church and that fellow parishioners had become like a family. The father reported that their fellow parishioners had offered food, emotional support, and a substantial cash contribution to their baby's funeral expenses. Another couple found support within their congregation when their minister introduced them to other bereaved couples. One couple in particular became and remained their close friends.

Some parents had to search for this support. Because of a lack of support from the parishioners of the church they attended when their baby died, Adam began to question his religious beliefs, to read the Bible on his own, and to have discussions with his pastor. These discussions made him realize that he and the pastor were on "different wavelengths." Adam and Lynn began attending another church and found a great deal of support there.

> I know that if I called now and said I have a problem, I know that there are three or four people who'd be coming through that door pretty quick. [Adam]

No Support and Negative Support

Seven couples who indicated membership in a specific congregation did not mention having received any support from fellow parishioners. In addition, three couples or individuals indicated either negative support or support that was not as high in quality as they would have preferred.

As noted above, Adam and Lynn did not find their church to be supportive, and so they changed churches.

> We were going to another church at that time [when the baby died]. There didn't seem to be anybody there that would say anything or do anything that was appeasing in any way. [Adam]

Dolores said that fellow parishioners had prayed for them, but she was surprised that these individuals remained anonymous.

> I know we had a whole bunch of people praying for us at church, but I don't know who they are. I thought they would come up and say, "Hey, I was praying for you." Nobody ever said anything . . . I had to bring it up on my own. [Dolores]

Religious Faith

For some couples religious faith was intertwined with the support they received from fellow parishioners. One couple who had been well supported at church reported that they became more active in their church after their baby's death, and two couples who also had been well supported indicated that their religious faith had grown. Two wives, neither of whom mentioned having received support from fellow parishioners, indicated anger at God or feeling punished by God.

Six couples and one wife indicated that religious faith had provided solace for them throughout their ordeal. Jonathan specifically mentioned his religious background:

> You think in terms of, "She's in a better place now than she ever would've been here"—but we still would've liked to have her here.

Asked where she found support, Susan mentioned her religious faith after discussing the help her husband, family, and friends had given her. Her husband, Ed, agreed:

> I don't know how anyone could get through a session like this without having some faith.

As noted in Chapter 3, an interpretation of their baby's death that involved a kind, loving God was helpful to individuals in this study. In all but one case, when one spouse indicated the importance of religious faith, the other spouse did also. Some couples mentioned praying together; also specifically mentioned was "rededicating our lives to the Lord."

For one husband, the baby's death led him to identify himself as a member of his wife's church. He began attending his wife's church and stopped attending his own. He told us that his religion was now the same as his wife's, as a result of changes that had occurred in him since his baby's death. His wife, however, although she mentioned that he was now going to church more often with her, stated that they had different religions. Thus, the husband, without his wife's knowledge at the time of the interview, had joined his wife in a religious sense by becoming in his own mind a member of her religion.

In summary, some of the bereaved parents in this study found support from fellow parishioners and from their religious faith. The death of their baby caused a number of parents to examine their religious beliefs and practices. For a few parents, this examination led to a change in the church that they attended or a rededication of their lives to God. Most of the parents who mentioned their fellow parishioners reported having received positive support from them. Religious beliefs were problematic if God was conceptualized as just and punishing. A few couples, however, found solace in their belief in God as loving. For these couples, religion was a positive binding force between them.

SOCIAL SUPPORT IN THE WORKPLACE

Another system outside of the nuclear family unit that has an impact upon the bereaved parent's recovery is the workplace. When a pregnancy is lost, or when a child is born and becomes critically ill or dies, the employers and colleagues of one or both spouses must be informed. The mother must receive medical care for at least a few days following (and sometimes preceding) the birth or miscarriage, necessitating that her employer be informed, if she has one. If a critically ill child is born, both parents may seek time off from work to be with the child in the hospital. If the baby dies, funeral arrangements must be made and carried out, and mourning begins.

The length of time that is provided for mourning in our society is short. Even in the case of the death of an adult family member, Americans tend to believe in an extremely short mourning period (Davidson, 1979). Although some of our respondents reported work-related problems, in general colleagues and employers were perceived as helpful.

Positive Support

Fourteen respondents mentioned positive responses from colleagues or bosses. One father said, "My bosses were great," since they gave him two hours off per day so that he could spend time in the hospital with his dying infant. Several other fathers reported receiving instrumental support from colleagues or a boss. Money was collected at the workplace (in two instances by a colleague, in another by a boss), and one father who had just taken a new job was told by colleagues to take as many days off as he wanted and was assured by the colleagues that they would cover his assignments. In addition, another man's boss volunteered good advice, advising him to have a funeral so that people would know about the loss and give support. (A hundred people attended the funeral.)

Several wives and one husband specifically mentioned that going back to work was helpful, in that it provided structure to the day and an opportunity to concentrate on something other than the baby's death. Two of these parents (both mothers) noted that they were not very productive at work until about six weeks had passed, but that their colleagues were understanding.

Negative Support

Several of our respondents expressed disappointment that colleagues were unwilling to talk, and two additional individuals (one husband and one wife) expressed anger that colleagues said offensive things, such as, "She's better off dead," or expressing disbelief that a parent would actually have a funeral for a dead infant. Another woman was embarrassed by colleagues' well-meant attempts to express sympathy; she said that she did not know how to interact at work outside of a professional role. Another female respondent expressed anger that she and her husband had been cut off from social interaction by colleagues who were able to afford expensive restaurant dinners that the respondents could no longer afford because of high medical bills.

In summary, bereaved parents whose workplace provided positive support in the form of opportunities for sharing emotions, and instrumental support (and less frequently good advice, flexibility in work hours, and understanding or support) expressed appreciation of the individuals who helped them. No individual in this study reported a negative experience with a boss, and two men specifically mentioned that their boss had been supportive. Fewer respondents mentioned disappointment or anger at the hands of colleagues. Those who did mention colleagues generally desired the opportunity to share feelings with colleagues and receive a supportive response.

SUPPORT FROM SIGNIFICANT OTHERS

Interface Issues

The term "interface issues" comes from the family therapy literature and refers to an issue presented by a client that is similar to a personal issue of the therapist's. In the current context, an interface issue is an aspect of the bereaved parent's experience that has a highly charged emotional meaning for the family member or friend who might otherwise provide emotional support to the mourner.

Previous studies are somewhat contradictory regarding the salience of death of an infant or pregnancy loss to persons close to the bereaved parents. The death of a child has been found to be extremely painful to the bereaved parents' significant others (Klass, 1988), and the loss of a pregnancy may also be (Borg & Lasker, 1989). However, in the case of infant death, other authors suggest that it is difficult for friends and relatives to empathize with the parents because they never knew the baby (Peppers & Knapp, 1980b). It seems likely that when significant others have no investment in the infant, empathy may be low. On the other hand, if they do have a personal investment in the infant, they too are directly affected by the loss and may be unable to provide much support (Bugan, 1983). Previous research indicates that the amount of support that significant others are able to provide is related to the amount of stress they concomitantly feel (Eckenrode & Gore, 1981). Studying parents with children who were dying of cancer, Chesler and Barbarin (1984) found that friends of the parents experienced pain and grieving, which made it difficult for them to help the parents. Coyne et al. (1988) reviewed literature that indicated that emotional overinvolvement with a family member's medical problem often results in the provision of negative rather than positive support by the family member.

There is little research that deals with the burden felt by helpers when they are directly affected by a bereaved individual's grief. Blau (1973) asserts that widowed individuals receive little comfort from relationships with their children. She attributes this lack of solace to the structure of the parent–child relationship in adulthood; that is, adult children are obligated to their parents, but are not their parents' peers and cannot substitute for the missing spouse. Lopata's (1979) research suggests that adult children and their widowed mothers avoid sharing their feelings of grief in an effort to protect each other. Thus, it may be that bereaved adult children and their parents cannot help each other because they are burdened by their own grief (Morgan, 1989).

Fourteen of the bereaved parents mentioned that the baby's grandparents also were grieving. Husbands were especially likely to remark that their own parents also were hurting, but

that the topic of the baby's death was not discussed by the grieving father and his father.

> I think it affected my dad quite a bit. . . . When Jeff was
> in the hospital [my dad] went with us a couple of times
> and he only went into the nursery once and that was for
> about 2 minutes. . . . Now, I don't think it affected my
> mom as bad and Faye's mom but . . . It affected [her step-
> father] the same way it affected my dad. . . . [Faye's step-
> father] went and saw Jeff once. That was it. And he had
> chances to go see him again. [Patrick]

When the baby died, Patrick's family would not talk about it.
Patrick reported that they said things like, "Oh, well, you'll get
over it."

Several wives also mentioned an inability to discuss the topic
with their own parents or with both sets of grandparents. Rita
put it this way:

> It's interesting, my mom was the least helpful of anyone,
> because, and this was my opinion, I think it hurt her so
> much that she couldn't help me because she couldn't help
> herself. She's 66 years old and a part of her died too.

Melissa said that her parents had provided instrumental support around the time of the baby's death and funeral but in an
effort to avoid the situation had left town for six weeks immediately following the funeral.

On the other hand, some parents reported that their grieving
relatives were able to openly share their own grief. Matt said
that he could share his grief with his wife's parents, and Charlie
said he could share his grief with his own parents. Four wives
mourned with their own grieving parents, although Monica
found her mother's concern to be excessive:

> My mother . . . had been given DES when she was preg-
> nant with me. I think she was, still is, overwhelmed by

guilt, thinking that the incompetent cervix, sometimes can be the result of the . . . DES. . . . I think that's why . . . it was hard for her, too. She was dealing with her own problems there and her own . . . grief with that whole situation. So, for her to deal with mine was tough.

Another wife described her mother's loss of the wife's baby brother, who died when the wife was six or seven.

I remembered how my mom, at the funeral and everything, how she handled it, and still, to this day, when certain dates come around, our whole family goes through the, like shadow grief. [Lynn]

Lynn described her relationship with her mother as extremely close, like sisters. She shared her mother's grief over the loss of her mother's son, and her mother shared her daughter's grief as well.

Jane was similar to Lynn in that she had a very close, empathic relationship with a female relative, in this case a twin sister.

I got an awful lot of support from my twin sister. It wasn't her child, but it might as well have been because she hurt as much, and in some ways, maybe more, because she could only guess the living hell that I was going through. And we are identical. And what happens to one, eventually will happen to the other. [Jane]

To summarize the information on interface issues, roughly a quarter of our respondents indicated that family members (usually their own parents) were also grieving about the baby's death. Of these individuals, about half said that they could not share mourning with family members, and the other half indicated that they did mourn openly with their relatives. Those who could mourn with their relatives felt very supported by this sharing. Some of those who could not share mourning seemed hurt by the lack of sharing, and others seemed to understand their parents' inability to mourn with them.

Positive Support

In this section, we consider the positive impact on the individual parent by extended family members and friends. An individual who has suffered a major undesirable life event such as pregnancy loss or infant death needs both material (instrumental) and emotional support. Caplan (1974) writes:

> Significant others help the individual mobilize his psychological resources and master his emotional burdens; they share his tasks; and they provide him with extra supplies of money, materials, tools, skills, and cognitive guidance to improve his handling of the situation. [p. 5]

INSTRUMENTAL SUPPORT

Family members, friends, and neighbors are called upon to give instrumental support, that is, the provision of goods and services (Cobb, 1982). Older children must be taken care of and provided with as normal a routine as possible while the mother gives birth and recovers, and/or spends days in the hospital with a critically ill infant. In the case of abnormal deliveries and the use of intensive care facilities, astronomical hospital bills may call for outside financial support as well.

One or both members in 21 of our 27 couples specifically mentioned that family members and/or friends had supplied instrumental support. At least one member of 19 couples reported receiving instrumental help from family members; at least one member of 13 couples reported receiving it from friends. There were five couples in which neither spouse reported receiving instrumental help from family or friends. Of

these five couples, three reported being supported in an unspe-
cified way by either family, family and friends, or friends.

The most common form of instrumental support, not surprisingly, was bringing food to the family following the birth or
death of the baby. All couples who had older children also mentioned that a relative, or less usually, a friend, took care of their
older child or children. Other instrumental help included helping to plan or carry out the funeral and postfuneral gathering,
going grocery shopping, inviting the couple for a meal, providing the parents a place to stay close to the hospital in which the
critically ill baby was staying, packing up the nursery, and providing money, usually to help defray funeral expenses. For
example, Susan's parents and siblings helped by taking care of
their older children when she miscarried and later went back
to the hospital for a D&C:

> [Family members] were real helpful like that, as well as
> friends, the girls I teach with, like bringing in food, I mean
> we had so much food. . . . Swinging by and picking up
> the kids and taking them for an ice cream cone . . . to just
> give Ed and me a little more time to deal with it ourselves.

In Ed and Susan's case, extended family members lived locally,
making the provision of instrumental help fairly easy. But even
couples whose families lived out of town usually received offers
of help from the relatives. For example, Gordon's mother drove
for eight hours to reach her son's home, and stayed for six
weeks.

Only four of the couples reported receiving no instrumental
help from family members or friends. In several cases, at least
one set of grandparents did not live locally. In another case, relationships with both sets of parents appeared to be strained.
However, it is not clear why these four couples did not receive
instrumental support from their friends. In at least some of
these instances, it seems likely that the nature of the questionnaire may account for the apparent lack of instrumental support
received. The couples were not specifically asked about instru-

mental or emotional support, but instead were asked who gave support. Thus, instrumental support may have been given in these four cases, but the respondents may have interpreted the question to mean emotional support.

EMOTIONAL SUPPORT

People who have experienced undesirable life events such as bereavement are in special need of reassurance and support from others (Wortman & Dunkel-Schetter, 1979). They need contact with others who have experienced a similar loss and the opportunity to ventilate feelings (Lehman, Ellard, & Wortman, 1986). Victims need to rebuild a conceptual system which allows them to see the world as not entirely malevolent (Janoff-Bulman, 1985).

According to Peppers and Knapp (1980b), the successful accomplishment of grief work requires the support of the community, which means all persons who have contact with the bereaved individual. The bereaved parent's "feelings of resentment, hostility, anger, guilt, and loneliness [must be dealt with by the parent] in a realistic, nonfantasy way" (p. 141). Peppers and Knapp maintain that it must be someone outside of the immediate situation who helps the mother to, in essence, rejoin the world of the living. "The community should act as a sounding board against which she can 'bounce' her emotional feelings, concerns, and sentiments; it should offer important feedback that can help her fit together a new perspective and resolve her grief" (p. 141). Thus, it is the parent's larger support system that helps the parent to rebuild his or her assumptive world (Parkes, 1972).

At least one member of 13 of the couples indicated that their families had provided emotional support, and an additional husband and four wives indicated that their families had been supportive without indicating whether the support was emotional or instrumental. Twelve wives, two husbands, and three couples indicated receiving emotional support from friends. One husband said that friends were supportive without indicating how. In addition, seven couples and six additional wives attended support groups. Three of these couples and five wives mentioned that a support group such as Compassionate Friends supplied emotional support. (There were, however, five couples neither spouse of whom mentioned receiving emotional support from either family or friends.)

The quality of emotional support that was reported varied considerably. Monica was grateful that

> our families just didn't interfere, I mean, they weren't a negative influence so we weren't being torn apart by any in-laws or that sort of thing.

At the other end of the spectrum,

> Our families were tremendous. Both of our families are here in town. Most of our brothers and sisters. That was our main support. Our families were with us all of the time, helping us, talking with us, just listening to us. [Diane]

Friends who were especially helpful were those who had had similar experiences of pregnancy loss or infant death. Several mothers commented about the uncanny way that, following their own loss, they suddenly ran into many other women who had had similar experiences. For example, Willa said that such a woman, whom she had known only slightly, called her after Willa's loss.

> We cried on the phone together, helping each other along.

In other cases, the bereaved parents were referred by a mutual acquaintance to another parent or couple who had suffered a similar loss. In Mason and Nancy's case, it was their minister who introduced them to two other couples whose babies had died. It was a friend of Gail's who introduced her to another woman whose baby had died.

We shared some of our crazy moments.

Most of the participants in this study indicated a need for validation of their experience by others. This validation could be supplied by their spouse, by a doctor or nurse, by family members, or by friends. However, for a minority, this kind of validation was found only in a support group.

As noted previously, eight of the couples specifically mentioned a support group as providing significant emotional support.

It was going to our support group and realizing we were not going nuts. [Kay]

Negative Support

Many of our respondents at one time or another were the recipients of negative support. In most cases, it appears that the providers of negative support did not intend to be hurtful, although there were incidents that seemed to involve malice.

RETICENCE ON THE PART OF RELATIVES AND FRIENDS

Nine respondents noted that friends and especially relatives were unwilling to talk with them about the death of their child or their pregnancy loss. Sometimes, friends would try to be supportive, such as friends of one couple who asked them out to lunch but then would not talk about the stillbirth. Although she was describing the way her friends at work behaved, Lynn's remarks are typical of the comments made by both mothers and fathers regarding friends and family who would not talk about the baby:

For as many years as I worked there and as close as I was

to some of those people, they didn't know what to say. And the thing was, I wanted to talk about it. [Lynn]

Many of the bereaved parents seemed to be aware that it was family members' and friends' discomfort or feelings of grief that resulted in their unwillingness to talk about the death. Some of the parents were also uncomfortable, such as one couple who did not want their parents to come from out of state to the funeral, or another woman who did not want sympathy from colleagues following her miscarriage.

HURTFUL COMMENTS

A number of parents (more likely to be women than men) reported that others made hurtful comments to them about their situation. Such comments are widely cited in the literature (Borg & Lasker, 1989; Klass, 1988; Peppers & Knapp, 1980b). For example, Kay was told by a friend, "You'll get over it." Following a premature labor, Melissa was told by her mother-in-law, "My feeling is you've never really been healthy." Lehman et al. (1986) studied individuals who had experienced the death of a child or spouse in a motor vehicle accident, and asked them about things that others had said that were not helpful, in spite of good intentions. They found that "the four support tactics most commonly identified as unhelpful were giving advice, encouragement of recovery, minimization/forced cheerfulness, and identification with feelings" (p. 442).

Why it is that alleged helpers make such hurtful comments is not known. Lehman et al. (1986) also asked a control group (individuals who had not experienced such a death) what they would say to someone who was so bereaved. The control group's answers revealed that they *did* know the kinds of responses that were helpful and not helpful. However, 20% of the control group spontaneously said that they would be anxious or nervous if they were called upon to express sympathy to bereaved relatives. Lehman et al.'s research suggests that it is nervousness, rather than ignorance, that is to blame for thoughtless remarks that are made to bereaved individuals who have suffered the loss of an adult child or a spouse.

Another possible reason for hurtful comments is that victims are seen by others as responsible for the unfortunate event (Janoff-Bulman, 1985), especially when victimization happens a second time (Silver & Wortman, 1980). In order to function in everyday life, people need to have a feeling that life is just and that bad things are unlikely to happen (Janoff-Bulman, 1985; Wortman & Dunkel-Schetter, 1979). Therefore, if something bad happens to another person, it is logical to assume that that person somehow brought it on. By avoiding similar behavior, others can assume that they will avoid becoming victims.

Our data unfortunately do not tell us why persons who have experienced pregnancy loss or the early death of their infants are so often the victims of damaging remarks. We suspect that it is a combination of anxiety and a lack of awareness of the impact of the loss on the bereaved individuals. Several respondents mentioned that they had been warned, either by a doctor, social worker, or other helper, of the kinds of hurtful comments that others would make. "Forewarned is forearmed" seemed to apply to these parents.

MALICIOUS COMMENTS

In a few instances in our research, it appeared that the bereaved parents were victims of malicious intent by significant others. In both cases, the mothers had either an extremely difficult situation following the infant's death or a pronounced grief reaction. In the guise of friendship, a friend offered to go shopping with Terri about six months after Terri's baby's death. But there were some conditions. Terri recounted her friend's words:

> "If you're going to be sick, I don't want to go. I really don't want to go out and have you get sick on me. And I don't want to go shopping at [a nearby] mall. I want to go to [a mall 60 miles away]. . . . I don't want to go to some dreary little restaurant because that's all you can afford. I want to

go someplace nice where I can have a nice brunch." And there's more! I couldn't believe it! "I don't want you to whine because you don't have any money and can't buy anything."

In the second instance, Gail's husband's sister, with whom Gail had had problems since the beginning of their relationship, wrote letters to the bereaved mother detailing the developmental achievements of her own baby, who was around the same age as Gail's baby would have been. In both of these cases, the friend or relative of the bereaved mother seemed vicious in intent to the mother. Because we interviewed only the parents and not members of the support system, we do not know if the perpetrators intended to be malicious. It does appear that in these cases the bad relationship between the perpetrator of the malicious comments and the victim predated the reported incident.

In summary, in the eyes of at least one of the partners, the vast majority of our couples were recipients of positive social support from friends and relatives. Instrumental or material support was most commonly given in the form of food, helping to plan and carry out the funeral, and taking care of older children. In most cases, this instrumental support was experienced as being emotionally supportive by the recipients.

Most of our respondents reported positive emotional support as well from family members and friends. Expressing and demonstrating sorrow, allowing the bereaved parent to talk and/or cry, and not expecting immediate recovery were experienced as emotionally supportive. Friends and relatives were cited about equally as givers of emotional support.

Negative support is support that, although it may be intended by the donor to be helpful, makes the recipient feel hurt or angry. Refusal to talk about the baby's birth or death or the parent's feelings, expressing views that do not coincide with the meaning that the parents attribute to their infant's death, and a general lack of supportiveness were the kinds of negative support most frequently mentioned. Family members were most frequently mentioned as givers of negative support, followed by friends.

CONCLUSION

This chapter provides a description of social support, both positive and negative, that was received by our respondents. More wives reported receiving instrumental support from their families and emotional support from their friends than did the husbands; husbands and wives were about equally likely to report receiving emotional support from their families and instrumental support from their friends.

In the next chapter, our respondents make suggestions to others who are involved with bereaved parents. Our respondents emphasized the importance of medical personnel's responses to them. They also made suggestions for family members, friends, and other bereaved parents. Finally, we make additional suggestions to medical personnel based on general findings from the study.

8

Suggestions for Professionals

I cannot imagine any place in the world that we could have had better medical and psychological care. How those people deal with it day in and day out, I have no idea. [Jonathan]

It's normal to hate your doctor. Everybody hates their doctor. The doctor is the only one that comes out of this ahead. The doctor and the hospital. They always get paid. The only hostility I feel is toward the hospital and the physicians. That's not rational. They really did the best they could. [Henry]

THE PARENTS' SUGGESTIONS FOR MEDICAL PERSONNEL

Virtually all of the bereaved parents in our study who were cared for in hospitals with major neonatal facilities were grateful for what they considered to be professional, compassionate care from the doctors and nurses. The exceptions were parents who considered the baby's death to be wrongful (for example, when the baby contracted spinal meningitis, allegedly from the infant in the next incubator). Parents generally had more complaints about small-town hospitals, although most of these parents recognized that the medical personnel there were not experienced in dealing with neonatal death.

136

They did not deal with us on a real personal level [at the local hospital]. We were in the waiting rooms and it seemed we were there for a long period of time. . . . We weren't getting progress reports or anything as to how he was doing. . . . I don't know if they were uncomfortable with it, which I'm sure they were, but there at [the other hospital] anything you wanted, they told you. [Melanie]

And in some cases, medical personnel in smaller hospitals also were given kudos.

We specifically asked our respondents for suggestions that they had for professionals, for family and friends, and for other bereaved parents. In this chapter, we will describe the answers that our respondents gave to those questions, and make further recommendations based upon the findings reported earlier. Table 8.1 is a summary of the parents' suggestions.

Medical personnel are on the "front lines" of this family crisis. They usually are the ones who inform the parents about the fetal or infant illness or death. Our respondents overwhelmingly endorsed a "human" approach.

I do remember there was one nurse in the hospital who made all the difference going through the miscarriage. She had had a miscarriage three months before, and it was almost hard to believe, because she seemed to have accepted it so well herself. She could talk about it with us without being overwhelmed. [Roy]

Bedside Manner

BE HUMAN

A number of parents (both mothers and fathers) stressed how helpful it was when medical personnel shared their own emotions, shared relevant personal experiences, and seemed to be personally involved. As noted in the previous chapter, parents experienced this as priceless social support.

TABLE 8.1
Bereaved Parents' Suggestions to Medical Personnel

Bedside manner
  Share own emotions and relevant personal experiences
  Be personally involved and approachable
  Respect parents' feelings; be compassionate

Communication skills
  Listen
  Solicit parents' feelings
  Be direct but kind

Provision of information
  Explain physical conditions completely, simply, and accurately
  Keep parents informed of child's progress
  Provide resources list (e.g., books on the topic)*
  Tell parents what feelings and reactions to expect
  Give information about dealing with older children
  Tell parents about support groups

Things to do
  Nurses: Ask mother if she needs anything
  Give parents a sense of control
  Give mother a pot of flowers to carry as she leaves the hospital
  Realize that routine medical procedures frighten parents
  Do follow-up of parents
  Offer, but don't push, help

Things not to do
  Don't say insensitive things
  Don't unnecessarily raise parental hopes
  Don't leave baby to die in hallway*
  Don't send father out to wait with other expectant fathers when
    it is known that his baby is dead or in grave danger*

---

*This suggestion was made by one parent.

The neonatologist called, wanted to know how I was getting along. I only met him one time. . . . I can remember
turning to the neonatologist and saying, "Whatever you're
paid, you're worth it." And he looked at me [as if to say],
"What a strange thing to be saying." We talked about [it,
and I explained], "I wouldn't want to be in your shoes, to
have to tell [parents] their child has died, I couldn't take

it. . . . I don't care what you're paid; you're worth your weight in gold!" [Miriam]

RESPECT PARENTS' FEELINGS

Bereaved parents stressed the importance of receiving empathy and respect for their feelings from medical personnel. Doctors and nurses should not impose their own feelings on the bereaved parents. If the parents need to cry, let them cry.

Several of the parents who were cared for in a university hospital noted that the medical students showed no concern for their feelings, instead crowding around and exclaiming surprise at the anomaly exhibited before them.

And the medical students, in particular, were really lousy. I don't particularly blame them. They're students and they don't know what they're doing. [Will]

Although the parents expressed tolerance for the students, it seems to us that greater effort could be put into extracting tactful behavior from medical students.

PROVIDE FOLLOW-UP CARE

A few parents mentioned that a physician had called them during the month following the baby's death to ask how they were doing, or had scheduled a follow-up visit. Charlie, for example, said that the follow-up visit was particularly helpful to his wife, who had not been present when the doctors explained their son's problems to him.

Communication Skills

Closely related to "bedside manner" are communication skills. Our parents enjoined medical personnel to listen to bereaved parents. Nurses and aides should listen when doing routine care of the mother. Doctors should listen when the parents have fears, concerns, or questions.

> I think too many people aren't able to deal with it, don't heal because their doctors, for instance, don't even let them talk about it. [Phillip]

Several parents wanted the doctors and nurses to help the parents with their feelings or ask the parents how they were. One wife thought that medical personnel should say, "Let's talk; tell me what your feelings are," but one husband said that medical personnel should realize that there aren't very many people "who'll come out and flat tell you about how they feel."

Another area of contradiction was how direct medical personnel should be in telling the parents about the impending death of the baby. Most of the parents who mentioned directness said that doctors should be "direct but kind." False hope should not be given to the parents. One woman, however, thought that the doctor was wrong to withhold all hope that her very premature baby would live. She wanted kindness but preferred the bad news to be given gradually. A number of parents who mentioned the importance of directness emphasized the importance of the manner of delivery of the message. Parents were grateful to doctors whose voices were "soft" and/or who prefaced the bad news with, "I am so sorry to have to be the one to tell you. . . ."

Provision of Information

It is the physician's role to provide information to the parents. The parents wanted doctors to explain physical conditions simply and completely, and to be accurate with medical information. The physician should keep the parents informed of the child's progress.

A number of husbands and wives received information from physicians and nurses about what to expect from each other, and from themselves. Parents were told to expect incongruent grieving.

> Maybe . . . the most helpful of anything they said to us was, "You're gonna grieve differently, and at times just understand each other and be patient with each other and try to help each other." I think that if Dr. Smith had not said that, I may have felt guilty for not feeling a need to go to [support group] and maybe Monica would have felt that I was not caring and not sensitive because I didn't want to go. So I think that that little instructional period right after the baby died is maybe as important as anything that happened to us. [Larry]

Several parents were also given specific advice about how to deal with their older child or children.

> And there was another pediatrician at that time . . . and he spent quite a bit of time with us, especially with me, discussing how to tell Caitlin [older child], what things not to tell her, and what things to tell her. That was helpful. At that time Caitlin was 3, and that anything you told her, she was going to take literally. So you couldn't say, "He's gone," because she'd want to know where he was and [would] want to go too. And you couldn't say, "He got sick and died," [because] what would she think if she got sick? She was gonna die . . . [Maeve]

Linkup with Outside Support

Medical personnel also are crucial links to outside sources of support. Parents should be told about support groups for bereaved parents. Specifically, the parents should be given information about when and where the nearest support groups meet.

Nobody hears about the support facilities that are available. Nobody hears about them unless a woman who has lost a baby meets another woman. It's even worse from the physicians, not exchanging information between disciplines. [Henry]

One couple even thought that someone should *take* the parents to the first meeting of the support group.

Additional Requests

Medical personnel should be direct, but give parents a sense of control.

Give [parents] a chance and let them feel they have a sense of control. [Lisa]

Parents need information about their options, but the final decisions about life-and-death matters should be left to the parents. For example, parents need to know what happens to fetal remains that are disposed of by the hospital.

Several parents expressed gratitude that they were given the opportunity to see or hold their dead baby.

One of the things that, at the time, it kind of got me or shocked me, but we went ahead and done it and then felt better, felt that it was the right thing, was after Peter died, they came out and told us that if we'd like to see him, that we [could]. . . . We were really glad that we did it and I think it was probably a good thing as far as finalizing things.[Charlie]

At the time of the baby's death, parents may be too overwhelmed to consider that at a later date they may want a picture of the baby. We advise hospital personnel to take photos of all babies and offer them to the parents. If the parents do not want the photos at the time of the infant's death or stillbirth, the photos should be filed and parents informed that if they change their minds, the photos will be available to them.

Doctors should become informed about parents' reactions to their baby's death. They also should realize that routine medical procedures frighten patients and their families.

> One of the nurses, I didn't think, was too good. The day they were doing a routine tracheostomy on Connie to see if that would help her breathe, I was really worried and I was really depressed, you know, cutting a hole in my daughter's throat with all her problems, you know, putting a piece of plastic in her neck. But they said, "I know you're worried, but this is routine. You know, there's nothing to worry about." Well, to me, "That's my kid! I'm worried whether you like it or not." [Kelly]

A number of parents made suggestions of things that medical personnel should *avoid* doing. Parents did not appreciate being told that they could just have another baby.

> Don't barge in and say, "Maybe it's for the best." God! So what if the lady's got three kids at home. . . . Watch what you say to somebody who's going to lose her baby. . . . [Don't) whip in and deliver this baby and disappear. You could say, "I'm sorry that your baby is not going to live." [Jennifer]

Jennifer's husband Matt saw their very premature baby in the hall outside the delivery room, with no one attending it. Jennifer suggested that

> If [a] baby is born alive, don't leave it to sit in the hallway to die. I think that OB men ought to have some sense . . .

One father complained that when his wife was in labor delivering a fetus that was known to have severe birth defects, he had to wait in the waiting room with other expectant fathers for a number of hours. His pain and grief over the loss of his baby were compounded by having to pretend to happily expectant strangers that everything was all right.

In summary, in the opinion of our respondents, medical personnel should have the dual role of providing accurate medical information and sensitive, humane care. They clearly rejected the idea that medicine is mainly the application of technology, and wanted the practice of medicine to involve a large measure of psychological care. While realizing that dealing with death and grief is stressful for professionals, the bereaved parents felt entitled to sensitive treatment.

Specifically, they wanted medical personnel to listen to them, share their own emotions of grief or sadness, and to respect the parents' feelings. Accurate medical information was to be presented clearly and directly, but with kindness. They felt that information about incongruent grieving and peer support groups should be given to bereaved parents.

PARENTS' SUGGESTIONS FOR FAMILY AND FRIENDS

We also asked our respondents if they had suggestions for family members and friends. We report their answers here because we believe that medical personnel may be able to help other concerned individuals to deal with bereaved parents, and because some of our respondents stated that medical personnel had prepared them for the reactions of family members and friends.

Not surprisingly, bereaved parents desired the same humane treatment from their friends and family that they did from medical personnel. Table 8.2 lists the suggestions that bereaved parents made for family and friends.

The most frequently mentioned requests were that friends and family listen and be available. Parents wanted family and friends to be open to discussing the baby, rather than attempting to avoid the topic. If they did not know what to say,

TABLE 8.2
Suggestions for Family and Friends

Communication
  Listen
  Be open
  Be tactful

Specific communication techniques
  Use child's name*
  Say you're sorry*
  Don't say, "It was God's will," etc.
  Don't say, "Baby would not have been normal"*
  Don't belittle grief
  Don't make Mom feel there is something wrong with her
  Ask to see pictures, footprints, etc.*
  Admit that loss has affected them (family)*

Being supportive
  Tolerate bereaved parents' bad mood
  Be available
  Call them
  Be loving; don't avoid; act normal*

Providing instrumental support
  Cook, do housework*
  Screen bereaved parents' mail*
  Ask, *What* can I do?*
  Take older children so parents can be alone

Respecting autonomy of couple
  In-laws shouldn't run things*
  Realize that even if parents cry, they won't fall apart*
  Parents need to feel they're in control, but people who have been
    through it before may be able to help them see things more
    clearly
  Don't question couple's judgment or decisions
  Don't push them to go to a party, etc.

Additional suggestions
  Acknowledge anniversaries*
  Send flowers and cards*
  Come and leave, don't stay long*
  Bring own babies over*

*Indicates that this suggestion was made by only one parent.

the best thing was to say, "I'm sorry," and try to take cues from the parents. Although some parents received solace from others' attempts to find religious meaning in the baby's death, it is safer for others to avoid making remarks such as, "It was God's will," unless the parent has already made it clear that that is what he or she believes.

Bereaved parents wanted family and friends to show understanding that the parents were experiencing grief. The parents wanted tolerance for their bad moods, the recognition that crying is normal and does not indicate mental instability, and the freedom to make their own decisions about the baby and their own behavior, such as whether or not to attend parties or family gatherings.

A few parents mentioned specific things that family and friends could do to be helpful, such as asking what needs to be done, doing housework and caring for older children, acknowledging anniversaries of the birth or death, and sending flowers and cards. In other parts of the interview, parents (especially wives) mentioned that they did not want to be forced to be near the babies of friends and relatives, although many people mentioned that they were bothered by certain people's babies, but not others'. When asked specifically what family and friends should do, however, one father stated that they should bring their babies over. It was his belief that although somewhat painful, this would help the parents' healing process. To us, it seems prudent for others to ask the bereaved parents' permission to bring other babies over to their home, especially within the early weeks or months following the death of the baby.

BEREAVED PARENTS' SUGGESTIONS FOR OTHER BEREAVED PARENTS

Professionals who deal with bereaved parents would benefit also, we believe, from knowing the kinds of suggestions that fellow survivors have for the newly bereaved. Table 8.3 provides a summary of the suggestions that our respondents made.

Whether or not they felt satisfied with their own communication process as couples, our respondents advised other bereaved parents to communicate with each other.

TABLE 8.3
Suggestions for Bereaved Parents

Communication
    Talk about it; get it out into the open
    Listen to each other

Support for each other
    Respect each other's feelings
    Be tolerant
    Be nice to each other*
    Spend time together*

Outside support
    Get involved in peer support groups
    Talk to others who have been through the experience
    Get support from many people
    Get professional help if needed

Positive focus
    Look for the good things you have
    Don't dwell on it*
    Help others
    Go back to work; get involved in life

Solitary helps
    Cry
    Talk to yourself, God*
    Write things down
    Distract yourself*

Concrete things
    Name your child*
    Have a funeral
    Get a headstone
    Involve your other children
    Have another baby

Additional suggestions
    Do what you need to do to get through it
    Ask questions; demand answers; be assertive
    Take your time; be patient
    Realize that the pain does go away

---

*These suggestions were made by one parent.

Talk it out and give each other some slack. . . . A lot of women perceive that their husbands are not grieving [in the same way that the women] are grieving because [the husbands] don't talk about it or they don't cry or they don't want to walk around in visible mourning. I think you have to realize that you are two different people and you grieve differently and to allow each other that personal privacy. Not to judge how the other person feels. [Kay]

My wife talked to me quite a bit about it. And when I got through the holidays . . . I clammed up and it was like pulling teeth for her getting to talk to me about it. But finally, I did, kind of reluctantly, talk to her and see how she was feeling and tried to comfort her. . . . Then the last three years, it was harder for me to. She had to pry more to get me to comfort her, probably more than she should [have]. And I can't tell you why I did that. It's just the way I handled it, I think. I didn't want to be bothered. [Patrick]

Along with communication, bereaved parents advised others to be tolerant of each other, and to respect each other's feelings.

Our respondents recognized that most bereaved parents cannot provide sufficient support for each other. Talking with other bereaved parents, either in a formal support group or outside of that context, was recommended by nearly half of the parents.

They need more support groups like Compassionate Friends. . . . One time, Jane and I flat out forgot the meeting. It seems like tension really built up [because] we missed that meeting. . . . We can really tell the difference when we miss a meeting. [Fred]

A few parents also advised that professional help is available for people who need it.

Several parents recommended a positive focus for bereaved parents, although other parents said that the newly bereaved should be patient with themselves and realize that healing takes time. Solitary helps, such as crying alone, talking to oneself, or writing things down, were recommended by a few. The observation of rituals such as a funeral and naming the child were mentioned by two parents.

In summary, the bereaved parents in our study made recommendations to other bereaved parents, the focus of which was on couple communication and the active solicitation of outside help, particularly from fellow survivors. Three parents summed up what parents should do by suggesting that bereaved parents should "do what they need to do to get through it."

SUGGESTIONS FOR MEDICAL PERSONNEL BASED ON OTHER FINDINGS FROM THE STUDY

Our findings suggest that parental bereavement following pregnancy loss and infant death does not follow clear-cut stages, but rather a series of overlapping phases. When examined closely, each individual's movement from one phase to another (and back again) is idiosyncratic. A contribution of this study is the examination of couples' grief processes, described in detail in Chapters 4 and 5. Parental grief involves each spouse's feelings and behaviors, and the reaction of each to the other.

Spouses should be told to expect incongruent grieving. That is, they should be told that each spouse will grieve differently, and that many different expressions of grief are normal. Part of the working-through process is dealing with one's own feelings about the other spouse's reactions.

Furthermore, each spouse reacts to the behaviors of others who attempt to help. Potentially, each member of each spouse's support network can start a ricochet of good or bad feelings. For example, the bereaved parent who feels injured by the comment of a well-meaning co-worker often turns to the other parent for support. The other parent, also burdened, may not be able to help.

"Forewarned is forearmed." Parents who were told early by medical personnel that they were likely to be subjected to outsiders' offensive comments seemed better able to frame the comments as awkward attempts at helping, rather than as painful assaults.

Conceptualization of the grief process as occurring at both the individual and the couple level should aid helping professionals in dealing with bereavement. Even when one spouse is clearly more directly affected by the death, the other spouse has to deal with his or her own feelings and behaviors and the feelings and behaviors of the other. Much tension and conflict come from expecting the other spouse to behave the same way as oneself.

CONCLUSION

When asked what suggestions they would have for professionals, friends and family members, and bereaved parents themselves, our respondents stressed open communication, support, and kindness. Medical personnel are usually the first people who deal with parents who are experiencing perinatal loss. Their behavior and remarks set the stage for what follows. Their kindnesses and their failures are remembered by the bereaved parents.

Medical personnel can provide information to the parents, not only a medical explanation of the baby's death, but information about incongruent grieving, the reactions of other people, and local support groups and other sources of help. Not all parents need support groups, but several couples in this study clearly suffered needlessly before learning about a support group.

Medical personnel can also help bereaved parents to understand that their grief occurs at both the individual and the couple levels. These parents must deal with their own responses, their spouses' response, and the couple dynamics that result.

The final chapter is directed specifically toward the helping professional. Information presented in earlier chapters is outlined and specific intervention tools are presented.

9

Support in Action
Helping and Healing
in a Time of Crisis

E. Britton Wood, Jr., Ph.D.*

A NOTE ON THIS CHAPTER

The following chapter by Britton Wood, Ph. D., a practicing family therapist and ordained minister, is directed to professionals whose clientele include parents who have experienced or are at risk to experience pregnancy loss or infant death. Such professionals include obstetrical and neonatal physicians and nurses, medical social workers, counselors, family and other therapists, hospital chaplains, and members of the clergy. Laypeople will also find here an essential, accessible perspective, which will help them both to assess where they are in the recovery process and to facilitate future stages of healing.

The chapter includes six checklists and open-ended questionnaires designed for use by professionals in their practice. All are based on

*Dr. Wood is a Family Life Consultant who works in the area of single-adult, marriage, and family enrichment with numerous institutions. His workbook on grief, *Survival Kit for Griefwork*, is used by institutions throughout the United States, Canada, and Australia. He and his wife are the president-elect couple for the International Association for Couples in Marriage Enrichment.

the findings of this book and on Dr. Wood's clinical experience as a grief counselor.

Table 9.1 is a checklist for medical personnel to use when counseling parents during the immediate bereavement period. Its purpose is to assure that parents are given crucial information in a timely fashion. Our findings indicate that this information plays an important role in the recovery process.

Table 9.2 is a questionnaire that medical personnel may employ to assess their own readiness to deal as professionals with parents who have experienced fetal loss and infant death.

Tables 9.3 through 9.6 are intended to be administered by counselors and therapists during grief therapy with bereaved parents. Table 9.3 is designed to help professionals assist bereaved parents' development of a healing theory at the individual level. Table 9.4 is intended to help bereaved couples recognize and reconcile differences in their respective healing theories. Table 9.5 deals with the emotional meaning of the baby's room. Table 9.6 concerns the parents' expectations for themselves and each other about their roles as husband and wife.

Dr. Wood also has provided the reader with a list of eight basic characteristics of normal grief (pp. 160–162) and the Wood Anger/ Emotion Agreement (pp. 169–170), a six-step process for using conflict constructively and creatively. Finally, Dr. Wood draws on his experience as a therapist and minister to underscore the uniqueness of this particular grieving process by briefly comparing the nature of fetal and infant loss with that of other types of loss.

INTRODUCTION

One of the important themes running through this volume is that often the people around the grieving couple are not sensitive to or do not understand the impact that the loss of a baby has on bereaved parents' lives. The authors of this volume have provided excellent insight into the dilemmas and concerns of these grieving couples. In this chapter, effort has been made to integrate the findings of Gilbert and Smart, and to provide a practical resource—a kind of "tool kit"—for the professional in relating to couples who have experienced pregnancy loss or infant death.

To relate wisely and therapeutically to parents after the loss of their baby is a delicate matter. When the professional has not experienced a similar loss, learning how to undergird the parents provides a window for the healing process in grief to commence. Social support comes from many sources and can be positive or negative. Facilitating the professional's understanding of what impact the kind of support given has on the bereaved couple is, in itself, instructional. As a follow-up to all that has been suggested to the helping professional, a checklist or a self-examination regarding how to relate to bereaved parents is provided.

Since the way parents "assumed" their world would be with their new baby has changed, they need to learn how to reconstruct an assumptive world that does not include this new baby. Information and facts about "normal" grief provide an avenue for the parents to face their own grieving situation more realistically. A readiness primer for assisting the bereaved parents draws elements of the grief theories together and helps professionals review concise information in order to administer the healing-theory questionnaire to each bereaved parent. An additional tool that draws information from the individual healing-theory questionnaires is provided in the Family Healing-Theory Form.

Once the parents have given voice to their healing theory, they can move further into their processes of healing. Getting in touch with each parent's emotions and negotiating an agreement for anger and other emotions becomes a necessary ingredient to the process. The parents may then have the courage to attempt an exercise that deals with baby's room.

If the professional has, with care, guided the bereaved parents in the healing process, consideration can be given at this point in the grief therapy to the reestablishment of the marital relationship, which includes the loss of the baby. Couple exercises are provided to facilitate learning for the parents and the professional. Through these exercises, the bereaved couple can become aware of the differences in their experience related to their gender roles, and differences in the way couples have chosen to relate to each other can be identified.

SOURCES OF SOCIAL SUPPORT FROM OUTSIDE THE MARRIAGE

Social support is described by Gilbert and Smart as behavior directed toward another person in response to the support-giver's perception of the recipient's needs. The recipient may perceive the support as positive (helpful or comforting) or negative (hurtful).

An example of *positive social support* is when the recipient feels loved, esteemed, and mutually obligated to other network members (Cobb, 1982). An example of *negative social support* is when the recipient receives a poor diagnosis from medical personnel or experiences comments and/or actions that are perceived as shallow, thoughtless, or lacking in understanding.

Most bereaved parents receive a mixture of positive and negative support. The first time a couple is given support (whether positive, negative, or mixed) is in discussions with medical personnel. This support usually is provided when the parents are given a poor prognosis for the pregnancy or the infant or when the actual loss of the baby occurs. A glimpse of the types of support that come from various social sources sets the stage for ably assisting the bereaved parents.

Social Support in the Medical Setting

Doctors and nurses are important sources of information; they are also potential sources of emotional support. Doctors and nurses are wise to keep in mind that positive support often comes in the form of information. Knowing what happened or what will happen to the pregnancy or the infant helps the parents deal with the reality of the situation. When information is given in a caring but straightforward way, it is perceived as emotional support by the parents. Parents will vividly remember everything that was done or said once the immediate impact of the child's death hits. It is important to recognize that parents will need help in handling this situation.

When I learned that a colleague's wife had a 13-week premature baby with many complications, I traveled 200 miles to see them. I sat with the new mother and heard in great detail all that the medical personnel had shared with the couple. I noticed that the new mother related both facts and her perceived understanding of the genuine care of the doctor. After I learned that the parents reacted positively to the way in which information was offered, I not only responded to the facts given but commended the medical personnel to the parents.

Bereaved parents need specific assistance when the shock of the loss of their infant is in process. The following checklist (see Table 9.1) can be used to ensure that the medical personnel includes the necessary items for the newly bereaved to consider.

To continue this discussion of positive support, a self-checklist is included for the medical person who works with couples who are becoming parents very soon or have an infant who has major complications. The Readiness Questionnaire for Medical Personnel (see Table 9.2) is for each individual who works in a medical setting.

Social support is usually available to the grieving parents from the clergy, fellow parishioners, co-workers, and significant others. See Chapter 7 for a fuller understanding of both positive and negative social support.

In my own ministry, I have found it important to respond to the question "why?" Parents grasp for answers. If they view God as *just*, they want to know "why?" Some parents are angry and feel ignored by God because their prayers have not been answered. With care and gentleness, I try to encourage them to feel what they feel. Be angry with God; he can handle your anger. If the question "why?" is valid (which it is), then one more question is equally valid, "why not?" If God is just (not the same as fair), then he is equally caring to all people. He does not select favorites. He has not "done" this to you to teach you a lesson. There are many factors to consider and the answer as to "why" is potentially unanswerable. The exact *cause* may not be found. God can help sustain parents in their loss. He will not abandon us. He can give us just enough strength for each difficult moment.

The four most common support tactics that do *not* help include giving advice such as: "What you need to do is . . ."; encouragement of recovery such as, "You'll be back on your feet in no time . . ."; minimization of or forced cheerfulness such as, "It's not as bad as all that, cheer up . . ."; and identification with feelings such as, "I know exactly how you feel . . . ." Another inappropriate comment that this writer has heard is, "You're young, you can have another baby."

Nervousness, rather than ignorance, contributes to the thoughtless remarks made to bereaved individuals. Sometimes, the assumption by others may be that the bereaved parents are basically responsible for the pregnancy loss or the infant's death—thus hurtful comments result.

Malicious comments often indicate the discomfort of the person making the comment with the current situation of the bereaved parent. In essence, things are different now. (Perhaps the person is grieving over the loss of his or her friend [the bereaved parent] whom the loss of the infant has changed.)

What then are some suggestions for assisting the bereaved parents to get on with their lives? How can the caring professional be constructively supportive in the process of their healing? It is important for the parents to reexamine their assumptive world.

The authors of this volume provide some excellent suggestions for parents to cope or reconstruct their assumptive world in Chapter 3. A brief reminder of each of them (plus some commentary) is beneficial at this point. Ways to cope include: (1) establishing a sense of structure; (2) gathering information; (3) searching for meaning; (4) blunting; and (5) sealing over.

Regarding "gathering information," besides learning from

TABLE 9.1
In Case of Fetal or Infant Death:
A Practical Sequence for Parents

COMPLETED

( ) 1. Funeral arrangements must be made by _____ (Date)

( ) 2. What cemetery plots are available:
a. Inquire of extended family members
b. Contact a funeral director (Ask medical social worker or hospital chaplain for a list of funeral directors.)

( ) 3. Provide a potted plant for bereaved mother to carry home from the hospital.

( ) 4. Fully inform parents of all specific data regarding the death of their infant.

( ) 5. The bereaved parents need to give each other permission to grieve uniquely.

( ) 6. Marriages often suffer after infant loss for various reasons, but a willingness to allow each partner to grieve in his/her own way can enhance the relationship.

( ) 7. The most appropriate professional needs to set a time with the bereaved parents to share "My Healing Theory"*
Date _____ Appointment _____

( ) 8. For the attending physician, it is most helpful to calendar in a phone call to the bereaved parents six to twelve months after the infant loss.

( ) 9. Encourage the bereaved parents to consider meeting with representatives from Compassionate Friends, SHARE, or other such bereavement support groups.

---

*"My Healing Theory" will be introduced later in this chapter.

the experience of others and the medical information, it is helpful for parents to learn what is "normal." What might a bereaved parent expect to happen regarding reactions and feelings? What information can be shared to help the bereaved parent gain a better understanding of the grief process? With respect to "sealing over," as the bereaved parent is able to give

---

TABLE 9.2
A Readiness Questionnaire For Medical Personnel
(Self-examination of My Perceptions of
Fetal Loss and/or Infant Death)

NOTE: Please ask all medical personnel who work with pregnant women and neo-natal care to complete this questionnaire for their own benefit. Awareness of self regarding the various aspects of emotions and issues surrounding potential and imminent pregnancy loss or death of an infant provides a self training tool for medically related individuals. (Each of the following numbered items needs these ☐ I can ☐ I cannot easily two choices in front of the number. All professionals can do a self-check regarding what they feel they can do with the parents. Self awareness of topics that are uncomfortable for the professional to deal with are important to identify.)

☐ I can   ☐ I cannot easily
1. Talk with the parents about some potential or apparent problems with the pregnancy or the infant.

   Preparation for the griefwork begins as soon as there is any clue that there are problems with the pregnancy or with the infant. Therefore, professionals in labor rooms need to bring up some issues. Not talking to the parents about the situation with their child leaves the parents to their own assumptions; that is "no news is good news."

☐ I can   ☐ I cannot easily
2. Ask the parents: Do you have any questions about this? Do you understand? How can I help you?

   Giving the parents the opportunity to raise any question or to express any feeling sets up the potential for openness in conversation and sharing at a later time.

---

a name to an issue or identify an unanswered question, it can be a beneficial tool in coping to mentally set up a "coping" filing system. Each issue has its own label and question(s) that are to be answered in time. As new information is realized or learned, it is placed in the appropriate file. When enough data are collected, the bereaved parent may want to examine the information. In essence, the serenity prayer attributed to Saint

☐ I can   ☐ I cannot easily
3. Encourage the parents to see and/or hold the body of their child.

Let them know the importance of the physical touch. Death is the close of a relationship. Closure is necessary and imperative for the loved persons—not seeing the baby's body can prolong and postpone closure.

☐ I can   ☐ I cannot easily
4. Inform the grieving parents that many of their family members and friends will not know how to be supportive to them.

It is not that they do not want to be supportive, but they often do not know how to be. It is not fair for the grieving parents to have to educate others—including grandparents—as to what to say and how to be of comfort. Many people—including grandparents—are at a loss as to what to say. They do not understand the impact of the loss of a pregnancy or an infant on the parents.

☐ I can   ☐ I cannot easily
5. Encourage the grieving parents to be patient with each other.

If married when infant death or pregnancy loss occurs, the way the couple has handled crises prior to the infant loss will be similar to the way they handle this crisis.

☐ I can   ☐ I cannot easily
6. Remind the grieving parents that this loss is both individual and relational.

Each person will grieve uniquely but the loss has an impact upon the marital system. It is difficult to say who has been affected more, mothers or fathers, but it is fair to say that each has been affected in his/her own way. How the grieving couple understands the uniqueness of their grief and the other person's grief will have much to do with their healing both individually and as a relationship.

Francis of Assisi best describes this coping strategy. The prayer text is: "God grant me the serenity to accept the things I cannot change, the courage to change the things I can, and the wisdom to know the difference."

The new continuity of meaning for bereaved parents cannot be programmed to fit into a neat time sequence plan. For example, friends and co-workers may give a father a day or two to grieve and then get on with life. However, stress continues to be present as a result of his maintaining the family, facing financial worries, needing to go to work, being expected to produce 100 percent, being the sole support to his wife, feeling isolated as a grieving person, feeling a need to handle the stress alone, and not adding to his spouse's stress. It is helpful to recognize that one person cannot make a relationship work, but one person can stunt or block the growth in a relationship.

There are often conflicts over grieving due to incongruent grieving. Instead of expecting the same grieving pattern from one's spouse, expect differences to be present. Give each other the gift of individual and unique grieving. What is normal for one may be very different from what is normal for the other.

NORMAL GRIEF

What is normal grief? After whom should each of us pattern our grief? How can I know that what is going on with me is normal? Sometimes I feel that I "ought" to be over some things and not be so emotional.

When a grief "wave" sweeps in on us, we can be overwhelmed. If we feel we ought not let that overwhelm us, we rob ourselves of learning more about what we are feeling at the time. We are wise when we accept the flow of grief as it comes. To fight grief is to force it away temporarily only to have it rush back at some unexpected time. Receive it as it comes as often as possible.

Normal grief has many levels and manifestations. The following comments should be kept in mind:

1. Normal grief is not tied to a fixed order of emotional states.
2. Normal grief appears to be related to the closeness of the relationship to the deceased and the perception of the preventability of the death.
3. Normal grief does not assume there will be resolution as in "When will I get over this." We don't get past this kind of loss, it becomes part of the "fabric" of who we are now. We

can never "get back to where we were before this loss." We can move to a different place. If we can get back to where we were, did the pregnancy or the infant mean much to us? The loss has made a significant difference in our lives.

4. Normal parental grief may become worse before it ever shows signs of healing. Often grief increases in intensity 6 to 12 months after the death.

    As a boy who wanted to ride his bicycle without holding on to the handlebars, I once had a terrible fall. My arms and knees were cut and my lips swelled up from the impact. When my mother saw me, she immediately began to clean the wounds with rubbing alcohol. It really burned and hurt more than it had before she started cleaning the wounds. If she really loved me, would she hurt me by cleaning my wounds? Yes, the only way healing could happen was to clean out that which would cause infection.

    Grief is the same way. We have been wounded. We need to clean out of our system that which is festering or contaminating the system. When we get the feelings out, it hurts—there is pain—but then a scab will form and we will have the illusion of doing much better. Then we will get the scab knocked off and it will hurt again. We discover again how tender everything continues to be. In time the protective scab falls away because it is no longer needed. Restoration is very near. However, a scar often remains.

5. Normal is normal for each person in its own way—no two persons grieve in the same way or at the same rate of healing. What is normal for one person is not necessarily normal for another. What one thinks or feels is normal for that person to think or feel. What one does with what one thinks or feels is where harm or health occurs over time.

6. Parents may fear "going crazy" because of recurring intrusive thoughts about their child. Does it not seem normal that a grieving parent will feel loss at major developmental stages of an infant's growth such as crawling, walking, saying "Mommy" or "Daddy," laughing, eating at the table, running, playing games, etc.

7. Normal grief includes the sharing of feelings, which is the best source of mutual support. Sharing of feelings also can bring about a most important result: mutual trust. Each parent may realize that "I feel affirmed and closer to you when you trust me with your feelings."

8. Normal grief recognizes that to gather in shared information will assist in mutual support. Facts do not change the situation, but they give the participants-in-grief the information that can help them realistically face the path ahead of them.

Each grieving person grieves in his/her own way (there is no standard way to grieve). An outgrowth of the grief process can be increased marital conflict, as many persons assume others will grieve in a manner similar to their own. Each grieving person is grieving and changing, not in the same way or at the same pace. Seldom are there mutually understood social rituals to assist the bereaved in infant death and particularly pregnancy loss. Unfortunately, grief is usually relegated to individual response. More attention and permission (by individuals and society) is given to the grief of the mother than to that of the father or couple relationship. Acceptance of however the grief process is expressed in one's spouse can strengthen the marital relationship.

Bereaved parents need to come to a point where each one can say, "We are on a road we did not choose, in a place we do not want to be, and we need to deal with the death of a loved person we had only just begun to love. . . ." They need to take responsibility realistically for the feelings they have by saying, "Now we are at a fork in the road, and we must choose the path we will travel from this point on. We choose what we become: bitter or better. It is our choice."

The helping professional can assist the bereaved parents to come to this place in their thinking and level of understanding. A wise step at this point is to provide the helping professional with a brief look at ways to assist the bereaved parents.

One of the most helpful ways for this writer to get ready to assist bereaved parents has been to determine a definition of grief, mourning, and bereavement. An excellent description of the various grief theories and definitions is provided in Chapter 2 of this volume. Grief is not easily categorized and labeled from within a person who is grieving.

Gilbert and Smart recommend the process approach that suggests a family paradigm and provides more fluidity. As this model includes a need for a healing theory, one has been designed to be used with bereaved parents. The recommendation is to ask each parent to complete the theory as fully as possible, separately from the other person. After each parent has written what he or she can, use the "Family Healing Theory" form (Table 9.3) to blend the thoughts on the "My Healing Theory" form (Table 9.4).

FOLLOW-UP SESSIONS WITH THE BEREAVED PARENTS

In the first session with the bereaved parents following the completion of the "My Healing Theory" questionnaires, the therapist will assist them in completing the "Family Healing Theory" form. Ask each bereaved parent to share or read what they have written on their individual questionnaires. Ask the other spouse to listen and write down what is said. When the sharing of the first reader is concluded, give the "Family Healing Theory" form to that reader and ask the other spouse to share. When both have shared and the ideas are recorded on the "Family Healing Theory" form, ask them to share with each other what they have observed. The value of this sharing is evident when each spouse hears the information as described by the other spouse as to what happened, how it happened, why it happened to me/us, why I responded as I did, what I would do if it happened again, and what I would want to say to my baby if I had the opportunity.

Once the therapist has led the grieving couple through the first eight points of the "Family Healing Theory," the next step may be to go back through those points and examine any aspect of either

---

TABLE 9.3
My Healing Theory: Helping the Bereaved Parent
Make Sense of the Loss of a Baby

My Name _____ DATE _____

My Baby Died on _____(date)

Recognizing both that the loss of a baby shakes one's assumptions as to how the world works and that each bereaved parent grieves differently from the other, the questions and statements listed below are intended to help you see what your Healing Theory is. Each one of us has one, we simply do not know what it is until a traumatic experience such as this one interrupts our lives. Please take the time to respond to each of the items below. Then, with your spouse, compare your responses on the Family Healing Theory Form.

1. Tell the story about the loss of your baby by completing the following:
   a. At what point did the loss of your baby happen?

   Pregnancy loss?

   As an infant?

   b. Describe the situation that resulted in the loss of your baby.

2. Have you experienced losses through the death of other significant persons in your life? yes ☐ no ☐

   Name of person   *Relationship*   *Date of Death*

---

spouse's response that needs clarification or affirmation. For example, look at the chronology and proximity of other grieving situations for each spouse (see Question 2) and ask the couple to comment on their relationship and any stress they felt during those grieving periods. Then the therapist can take the couple through the remaining segments of the "Family Healing Theory."

3. Are any of the feelings you feel now similar to the feelings you felt in any of those losses?

    If so, describe.

    If not, what is different this time?

4. What has surprised/pleased you about the way your spouse has acted/reacted to the loss of your baby?

5. Every loss has an impact on our lives. Please circle or check any feeling listed below that describes what you feel or how you have felt.

weird	confused	shut down	depressed
strange	numb	in a dream	aimlessness
unreal	out of synch	helplessness	frustrated
stunned	overwhelmed	out of control	angry
shock	disbelief	moving in a fog	fatigued
powerlessness		sense of unfairness	
going through the motions			

6. What other feelings (not listed above) have you felt?

7. Describe in your own words what the loss of this baby means to you.

8. Dream for a moment, describe what you imagine the future with this child would have been like.

Adapted and Designed by Britton Wood, Ph.D.

An important exercise the therapist can ask the couple to participate in is to share with each other what feelings each one heard the other emphasize (see Questions 5 and 6). Each spouse has a need to hear his or her feelings expressed and heard by the other partner. A way to accomplish this exercise is to ask each spouse to begin by saying, "I heard you say that you

---

TABLE 9.4
Family Healing Theory

NOTE:After each bereaved parent has completed the personal Healing Theory form, use this form to compare responses. Remember that any response given is appropriate and anticipate that the responses will be different from each spouse. Items 1 through 8 (Part 1) parallel the same numbers on "My Healing Theory" form.

Part 1

1. What are the details of your stories about the loss of your baby?

    Similarities in descriptions:

    Differences in descriptions:

2. Total number of significant losses (combine from both lists)

    Wife _____
    Husband _____
    Total _____

3. What feelings have you described regarding the other losses and the loss of your baby?

    Similarities:

    Differences:

4. Compare notes on your spouse's response to the loss of your baby.

    Similarities:

    Differences:

5. List all feelings (from the list) that each spouse has felt since the loss of your baby.

---

felt . . ." and to indicate each feeling that can be recalled. The follow-up question can be, "Have I accurately stated what you feel?" If so, let the other spouse affirm what was just said as correct or further amplify some feeling not accurately heard.

6. What are the other feelings each spouse has felt that were not on the list in question 5?

7. Compare what this loss of your baby means to both spouses.

8. What do you both think of when dreaming about your future with this baby?

Part 2

The following statements/questions concern your marital relationship. Please indicate where you are, as candidly as you can.

9. Given: Spouses have special power to validate or invalidate the beliefs and perceptions of the other. Underscore/circle your feeling.
   From my spouse . . .
   a. I feel assisted/impeded in my beliefs and expectations.

   b. I feel less stability/more stability in our relationship.
   c. I feel isolated from/together with my spouse in my grieving process.

10. Disharmony in marriage is normal for grieving parents. On the continuum below, where are you? (initial your response)

None_____ Extreme
       some   moderate   a lot

11. Who knows how one "ought" to grieve? What kind of grieving did you expect from your spouse?

   When you grieved, I expected you to . . .

   Actually, I would like for you to:
   ____stop feeling sorry for yourself
   ____move on
   ____stop avoiding your feelings
   ____grieve the right way, my way

Adapted and Designed by Britton Wood, Ph.D.

The number of sessions required to accomplish this process is unique to each couple.

IMPACT OF THE LOSS

Parental bereavement is a unique stressor in that it affects *both* spouses directly, *both* spouses indirectly, and the marital relationship. Where there is pregnancy loss, the mother often develops a stronger attachment for the baby than does the father. Conflicts over beliefs and expectations surface in unanticipated ways. The therapist may choose to encourage the grieving couple to keep a journal that includes a progress report on each partner's perceptions, feelings, and reactions to the loss—after one month, two months, three months, and up to the end of the first year. Over a period of time, the grieving parents can begin to see changes in their own perspectives or that they are indeed "stuck." To become aware of where one is contributes to one's healing process.

When a person grieves, it is normal to be preoccupied with one's own feelings. It is often quite difficult to provide comfort, support, and a willing ear to the other spouse. Many couples need assistance in learning how to handle or work through these periods of preoccupation. It can be beneficial for the grieving couple to come to an agreement regarding what to do with each partner's emotions, including anger, when they seem to be stuck. Designing and agreeing to follow an anger/emotion contract becomes a major step for couples to deal with the impact of the loss.

AN ANGER/EMOTION AGREEMENT

In this writer's marriage, the decision to agree on an anger contract has been a relational lifesaver. Not that divorce was nearby, but the fact was that neither of us had a family background that trained us in the sharing of feelings, particularly angry feelings. To come to an agreement on a list of ground rules for coping with the range of emotions has been the single most therapeutic process in enhancing our marital relationship.

Instead of viewing anger as an enemy to the relationship, it should be seen as a friend. Anger is the clue that there are deep feelings present that need to be understood by both persons so that the relationship can continue to grow. The result will be a mutual feeling of couple closeness and intimacy because "my" feelings were voiced and *understood* as were the feelings of the other grieving spouse. Intimacy is right around the corner from conflict if spouses will risk the full exploration of their feelings. Usually when a person shares feelings and also feels heard and not criticized, that person gains a sense of affirmation and a new level of trust, safety *and* intimacy emerges.

The following anger/emotion agreement is the one used by Drs. Bobbye and Britton Wood in their marriage relationship. Allow this agreement to be a model from which the bereaved parents design their own agreement. Each married couple needs to be on the same "page" and talk the same "language" when dealing with delicate issues like feelings.

THE WOOD ANGER/EMOTION AGREEMENT

1. Acknowledge your anger/emotion. Saying something like, "I am angry" or "I am feeling . . ." to your spouse begins this process. One aspect of this step is self-acceptance, acknowledging the fact that "I" am angry or have an unresolved feeling that needs to be shared and the right to feel that way.
2. Tell your partner that you are angry. It is one thing to acknowledge this feeling within, it is altogether another thing to tell the person you love that you are angry. (The goal here is to be heard and understood, not to have the other "fix" the problem or to feel blamed.)
3. Assume that one person cannot be fully responsible for the anger of another. Even if one's spouse has triggered the emotion or the anger "button," it is logical to assume that other elements from various persons and sources have contributed to the high level of emotion.
4. Agree to be non-harmful to each other in a verbal or a phys-

ical way; in other words, no abuse of any kind—verbal, physical, or emotional—no attacks on the person with critical or harmful words or mind games or violence. This step in the agreement reinforces the essential safety of this relationship to do any sharing deemed important by either spouse. What a freedom-building step this is!

5. Agree to a time to listen to the feelings of the angry partner that is fair to both spouses.

6. Allow the angry partner to share all the feelings possible without interruption. The silent partner is to listen attentively in order to give the sharing partner feedback as to what the listener heard. If accurately understood, then the listener becomes the speaker when all feelings have been shared by the angry person.

The Woods both agree that the ability to use conflicts constructively and creatively is the result of their involvement in the Association for Couples in Marriage Enrichment founded by David and Vera Mace. It was through their relationship with the Maces that they became aware of the concepts outlined in David Mace's book, *Love and Anger in Marriage* (1982).

Therapists can recommend that bereaved couples who want to continue to grow stronger in their relationships become involved in marriage enrichment, particularly in a marital support group. The Woods have been meeting with their marriage enrichment support group once a month since 1984. The purpose of this monthly small-group meeting is for couples to continue to work on their marriage. When couples engage in this kind of ongoing self-help group, the circle of support enlarges and the couple is helped to get into a growth mode again—or perhaps, for the first time. The Woods have produced a video on "How To Establish and Maintain a Marriage Enrichment Support Group," which is currently available to helping professionals.

When the grieving couple agrees upon the way emotions can be addressed in the marriage, a new vista of possibilities for each individual and for the relationship becomes evi-

TABLE 9.5
Getting in Touch With My Emotions—Baby's Room

The flow of emotions may cause grieving persons to move back and forth between one phase of the grief process and another.

Many of our emotions are held back because we may not know what to do with them. Discovering what we feel can assist us in the healing process. So, please do the following exercise as a way to get in touch with your emotions regarding Baby's Room. Most bereaved parents have made some space plans in their home for Baby.

Draw a floor plan of where you live. Indicate where the infant was to sleep. What can you do with that space? Look at each room in your home and indicate which room has warmth for you and which room seems cold or one into which you do not like to go. Simply write down information on this sheet where you wish. There is no correct way to do this exercise. Share what you have learned with your spouse.

dent. One possibility is that one or both parents need to get in touch with their emotions regarding the room they had prepared for the new baby in their home. The exercise "Getting in Touch with My Emotions" (see Table 9.5) is designed to address this issue.

RESTABILIZATION OF A MARITAL RELATIONSHIP

Open, supportive communication is usually the key to reestablishing the marital relationship as recovery from loss occurs. The ability to talk with one's spouse gives that person a sense of being connected and allows him or her to test and confirm growing healing theories. The exchange of accurate information has proven to be helpful in answering questions that couples have had about the death and each other. As one grieving spouse shared, "Seeing his pain . . . showed me he cared."

Listening is an important gift to one's spouse. If the listener feels the need to "fix" the pain of the spouse who shares, the stress of the listener is potentially increased.

Nonverbal communication has become an important way to share when direct language is difficult. Code words and signals become a type of shorthand that allows partners to communicate without letting others know.

Looking for the positive in each other and the relationship proves an important contribution to reducing conflict. Positively reframing the spouse's behavior is a helpful tool in altering the perception of the spouse's behavior. For instance, rather than saying, "You don't seem to care about what is going on with me these days," the sentiment can be reframed as, "At times I wonder if you become as preoccupied with our baby's death as I do."

Looking for the "in common" agreement areas often helps the couple to see the few disagreement areas from a healthier perspective. Sharing the loss with one's spouse helps both partners to see it as a mutually experienced loss. Learning to grieve together includes hugging and touching and some talking. This does not imply identical grieving, but it does mean being exposed to more information about the other's grief. Effort needs to be made to create exclusive time for each other. Priority time with no other obligations can be very helpful. Freedom from any other parental responsibilities for a few hours can be quite beneficial when used wisely.

Having something to focus on outside the marital relationship allows couples to work as a team. Whether that focus is the other children, other bereaved couples, the relationship itself, or the health of the wife (or the husband), to work on the area together can be helpful.

If decided on by both partners, common goals and common values allow couples to regain a sense of themselves as a couple. Deciding on another mutually agreed upon goal can be quite an accomplishment. However, settling on a common goal can be in itself a source of conflict.

As bereaved couples are sailing in uncharted waters together, flexibility or the ability to change course as needed becomes an important conflict reducer. However, it is helpful to remind each other that change can be difficult to adjust to after infant loss. The feeling might very well be, "Let *something* stay the same. I've had all the change I can take!"

Although difficult without good communication, acceptance of differences can be quite helpful in the couple's healing process. The sooner differences are accepted, the better able the couple is to deal with conflicts. One of the most important aspects of the acceptance of differences is for each spouse to know that it is O.K. to feel the way he/she feels and to have an anger/emotion agreement with the spouse. After all, if a spouse has to grieve in the "appropriate" way at home, where can he/she be truly him-/herself?

Each individual has a unique need for space. Partners who respect the spouse's need for space as different from their own will enhance the healing process of both.

Role flexibility or a willingness to make the family tasks an "our" responsibility rather than a "his" or "her" responsibility is extremely helpful to couples when one spouse is unable to share the load due to ill health or for some other reason. Flexibility in role performance provides yet another way for one spouse to assist the other in the healing process. It is something concrete that one can do.

Sensitivity to each other's needs contributes to the reduction of marital strain. When one spouse expresses a sensitivity to the other's needs and responds to those needs, the recipient is affirmed. When the receiving spouse confirms the awareness and the gratitude for the gift of sensitivity, both spouses benefit. Being thoughtful and being perceived as thoughtful is a wonderful love gift to the marital relationship.

Gender behaviors and expectations provide much of the frustration in marital relationships. Gender behavior training takes place during childhood and adulthood, but there seems to be no training for the husband and wife after the loss of a child through death. Silence usually reigns on the topic of what to do when one's baby dies. There is little or no guidance on specific behavior—particularly for gender role expectations. The exercise "Gender Role Expectations" (see Table 9.6) is designed to assist the couple in understanding more of the gender-role expectations each has for the other.

ACCEPTANCE OF EXPERIENCE RELATED TO GENDER ROLES

Men do not understand what it is like to carry a baby in the way the mother does. However, men *do* understand loss and they *do* care. Too often men are expected to be "healed" short term, whereas the women are given permission to take longer to heal.

Understanding Bereaved Mothers

A woman's expectations of herself as a mother usually includes carrying the baby to term. Miscarriage can represent a failure in gender expectations. If the baby died as an infant, the expectation of being a good mother and promoting health and growth would represent one's failure as a mother. These are heavy expectations for a woman to have—they are also self-imposed.

When a miscarriage or premature birth has occurred, women often feel betrayed by their bodies. A series of feelings can flood a woman's mind—a sense of failure as a woman, letting down a loved one, or feeling totally responsible, guilty, inadequate, incompetent, and at fault or to blame.

The feeling of inadequacy as a result of the pregnancy loss tends to foster a lack of confidence in becoming pregnant again—questioning the ability to bear children.

Inability to perform the role of wife can become difficult. There is often a tendency to think globally. Global thinking says, "I can't do anything right, I am totally inept." Instead of being situation specific, all aspects of one's life are poured into the same mixing bowl. No person does *everything* wrong. The

---

TABLE 9.6
Gender-Role Expectations Exercise

---

1. For which spouse do you think the loss of the baby is more difficult? ___wife ___husband

   Explain:

2. Understanding Couple Mourning Behavior.

   How are we "supposed" to act as a mourning couple?

   How long are we to be this way?

   When does the public mourning cease?

3. Some couples participate in competitive grieving. There can be a tendency to feel blame if the other wants something due to that spouse's mood. When your spouse says one of the following, What do you feel?

   When you say . . .   I feel . . .
   - "I need a hug."
   - "I should have known . . ."
   - "If I had only . . ."

4. Each spouse can benefit from a greater awareness of what he or she does for the other that will be appreciated. Complete the following sentence with your spouse in mind. "I feel understood or appreciated when you . . .

---

impact of the loss may be so great that some wives need their husbands to take over certain details of what they have traditionally done.

Some wives are able to be supportive of their husband's feelings by assisting them in their emotional expressions. Rather than taking criticisms and complaints personally, these wives recognize that their husband's complaints about minor things are, in reality, an expression of grief over the loss of the child.

Understanding Bereaved Fathers

Role ambiguity makes it difficult for grieving fathers to directly experience their feelings. The first double bind is to be strong and protective of your wife, but not to expect any support for your own grief. The second double bind is if you need to grieve, do it in an appropriate way—cry, be sad, and then get better. Men have traditionally been taught to "play with pain" in sports and elsewhere, and now they are told to cry and respond to the hurt and share feelings.

Focus on the wife affects the husband's healing process. Often a husband's grief is postponed because of the physical and emotional condition of his wife. Husbands are often called upon to be rational, have things under control, and to make decisions such as whether to view the baby and what kind of funeral or disposal plans should be made. As a result of the husband being charged with making many of these immediate decisions, the wife may not see him grieving. She may feel alone in her grief.

Men are often "avoiders" in grieving situations. They may use work and social situations as distractions or avenues of avoidance. Men seldom give themselves permission to be weak. They must be strong at all times.

Men tend to show anger more than do women. As anger is an indicator of another emotion and men have difficulty sharing their emotions, anger becomes a way of venting or releasing some of the internal pressure. Many times anger is understandable and warrants response. What is needed is for them to get in touch with what is behind the anger. To identify the emotion and the attitude behind the anger will open the door to healing. Social acceptance of men who show anger is more prevalent than acceptance of men who express sadness.

Contradictions or inconsistencies are often present in bereaved fathers. For some grieving husbands "taking charge as a man" doesn't mean fearing emotions. Communication doesn't always mean a great deal of verbal sharing. Many women value simple expressiveness in their husbands, yet many husbands understand expressiveness as "doing something" for their wives. Of course, some men are more emotional and expressive than their wives.

A certain role performance is often imposed on men, sometimes by themselves. Too often men feel it is their duty or role "to be responsible." Being responsible can be beneficial to the relationship when the husband also gives himself permission to still be in the grieving process.

Rather than ask the question "Shouldn't I be farther along in my healing than this?", a more helpful question may be "What can I learn about my feelings at this time?" Even to say "I'm still learning and healing," facilitates a better understanding of the husband's role. Male support systems are seldom available, and few men feel support from other men. Some men feel overburdened by the emotional needs of their wives. When compounded by financial problems, a man's emotional limits are severely tested.

A BRIEF COMPARISON OF GRIEVING SITUATIONS

As the helping professional provides guidance for the bereaved parents following the pregnancy loss or infant death of their baby, it is important to keep in mind the uniqueness of the loss of a baby. Babies are supposed to be born and grow up. Yes, babies can and do have complications, but they usually live. Infant death comes at a time when new life is welcomed by those close to the birth. The nature of this loss is tragically unique and totally unexpected.

Although it is not fair to expect bereaved parents to teach others how to relate to them, it often seems to be the best way to get some friends/family to open up. Friends and relatives may refrain from saying anything about the baby or the death because they are afraid of saying the wrong thing. After all, it may be the first time they have had to deal with people they care about losing a child through death.

When there is a death of an older son or daughter who is school age, the loss is great, but the awareness of many outside sources of potential harm are already known to the parents. An effort to provide safety is standard operating procedure for parents of school-age children.

The impact of the loss of an adult child is also powerful. The parents are joined by one or two other generations who suffer loss of a spouse or a parent. The parents of an adult child who dies or is killed often wish that the adult child could have been spared and the parent taken. The parents feel that the death of the adult child is not the "natural order" of things—parents should die first.

When a spouse dies, the loss is often quite devastating to the other spouse and to the adult children. The adult children have many new things in life yet ahead of them, but the parent will no longer be available to share in those things. The spouse who is widowed suffers from the loss of a life together that includes many memories.

Violent deaths are, by definition, unique. Murder, sexual assault, airplane crashes, fires, and hazardous vocations bring a different ingredient into the loss. Violent deaths are indeed violations. In these situations, death is not due to illness, emotional disturbance, or any other unprovoked source from within the person. These deaths demand justice. They are very difficult to work through and, more often than not, they have a dramatic effect on the survivors of the victim.

This brief look at loss through various types of death may help the bereaved parents following an infant death to see that when death comes—whether early or late in life—the impact upon loved ones is traumatic. However, there is some training in all families for death later in life, whereas there is seldom training through observation or experience for infant death. Grieving parents need special care and empathetic responses from those who tend to them as medical personnel, clergy, significant others, and family members. When the kind of loss the professional is dealing with is different from that person's own experience, it is good to review the various aspects of emphasis in this volume before talking with the bereaved parents.

CONCLUSION

Recognizing that each couple is unique when faced with the loss of a baby and that each bereaved spouse grieves differently from the other, sensitivity and understanding are imperatives for the professionals who relate to these parents. The loss of a baby in pregnancy or infant death is a traumatic experience that deserves more recognition. The findings of Gilbert and Smart attest to this fact.

The loss of a baby can be more traumatic when the couple has postponed marriage. The limitation of one's biological clock may initiate a more anxious attitude in the bereaved parents. The emphasis of success in business, in marriage, and in family can also contribute to the anxiety of bereaved parents. The simple fact is that when a loved one dies at the beginning of the life span, the loss is unexpected and unplanned. All plans included the coming of life, not the loss of life.

As helping professionals become more aware of their own limitations and preferences in responding to bereaved parents, they become better students of the grieving process. As these professionals identify their own feelings and tendencies, they can see where further training in relationship skills is needed. The careful blending of gentleness and forthrightness by the professionals closest to the bereaved couple contributes greatly to the healing process.

Appendix A
Methodology

THE QUALITATIVE APPROACH

In our data collection and analysis, we used qualitative methodology, which relies on verbal rather than numerical data and explores the symbolic or phenomenological aspects of life (Schwartz & Jacobs, 1979). These methods focus on process rather than outcome (Patton, 1980) and utilize inductive analysis in which abstractions are drawn from the data and are grouped together, rather than deductive analysis intent on proving or disproving research hypotheses (Bogdan & Biklen, 1982). LaRossa and LaRossa (1981) have suggested that a qualitative study may be the best way to conduct an exploratory study of social interaction.

According to qualitative researchers, each person views life from a unique perspective and focuses on different aspects of life. The holistic view of qualitative research facilitates the study of these differences (Bogdan & Taylor, 1975; Patton, 1980). Berger and Kellner (1964) have suggested that social life is the shared creativity of individuals, and Filstead (1970) has proposed that qualitative research serves to understand and explain the process of this shared creativity. We propose that the study of interactive bereavement in marital couples requires an understanding of both the subjective experience and this shared creativity; the qualitative approach is ideally suited to this exploration.

Qualitative methods are considered most useful in discovering and generating theory (Glaser & Strauss, 1967) and in the study of areas in which little is known (Lincoln & Guba, 1985; Patton, 1980). A careful review of the literature has shown that our understanding of the ways in which couples act as an interactive system as they resolve their grief is very limited and that efforts at grounded theory of this process have relied on data gathered from bereaved mothers (Peppers &

Knapp, 1980a,b). Because of this, not enough is known to legitimately delimit the study to an extent necessary for a strictly or primarily quantitative study. It is important at this early stage of theory development to have a clear understanding of the context in which the interactive recovery process exists, and qualitative research is best suited to this purpose (Guba, 1978).

Finally, this investigation is a study involving interrelated levels of analysis from a holistic perspective. Walker (1985) has suggested that, to understand the process of family stress, it is necessary to examine various levels of systemic functioning simultaneously. The study of complex family phenomena often involves multiple levels of analysis (Thompson & Walker, 1982), and the holistic study of different levels of systems is complicated by this. Yet, it is necessary in the understanding of multiple motivations. Walker (1985) has suggested qualitative methods as an appropriate voice in the study of family stress in the context of multiple system levels.

PARTICIPANTS

This study used a convenience, volunteer sample of 27 married couples who had experienced a fetal or infant death. All of the couples resided within a 200-mile radius of Chicago.

The age range for women was 26 to 42, with a mean age of 32.1; for the men, the range was 27 to 42, with a mean of 33.6 years. All respondents were white. Couples had been married from 3 to 14 years at the time of the interview, with a mean of 8.8 years.

Several occupations were represented for both women and men: Ten women were full-time homemakers, two were full-time students, 10 held full-time professional positions, two had clerical jobs, one ran her own full-time business, and two operated part-time or seasonal businesses. Among the men, the largest group, 15, held professional positions. Seven men represented skilled trades. Three men operated their own businesses. Two were employed in public safety positions. All were employed full-time.

Everyone had completed at least high school, and a majority of both husbands and wives had achieved at least a bachelor's degree. An equal number (10) of men and women had completed at least some work past the bachelor's degree. As couples, 11 wives had more education than their husbands, 10 wives had less education than their husbands, and in six cases, the educational level attained by marital partners was equal. In most cases where there was a difference in education level between spouses, these were small—for example, some college versus a high school diploma.

Catholicism was the most common single religion (22.2% of the women and 25.9% of the men were Catholic). A majority of individuals were members of Protestant denominations (59.7% of women and 63.0% of men). A small percentage were unchurched (11.1% of both women and men). None were Jewish. For couples, the most common pattern was for both the husband and wife to belong to the same religion (15). Partners in five couples were members of different religions, and in six cases, one person was a member of a religion while the other was unchurched. One couple was unchurched.

Nine couples reported the loss of more than one baby in pregnancy or infancy. Of these, five experienced two losses, three couples reported three, and one couple had lost four babies. These couples were asked to concentrate their discussions on only one of these losses, although they were not discouraged from discussing their response to their other losses.

Tables A.1 through A.3 summarize information about the babies these couples had lost. Table A.1 shows that nine of the losses were fetal deaths, that is, they took place before or during the birth; the remaining 18 were infant deaths. Of the nine that took place during pregnancy, three were early fetal deaths (up to the 21st week of the pregnancy), three were intermediate fetal deaths (21 to 28 weeks), and three were late fetal deaths (over 28 weeks). For live births, six infants lived less than one day, five lived from one day to one week, four lived one week to one month, four lived one to three months, and two lived over three months.

Time since loss ranged from one month to eight years for all losses and, as Table A.2 shows, six months to seven years for the losses that served as the primary focus of their discussions. Median time since loss was from two to three years before the interview date.

Table A.3 shows the cause of death. This was sometimes confusing, or, in three cases of fetal death, unknown. Often, parents were given only partial explanations, because no more information was available. Often, the cause of death given was a "best guess," based on symptoms. Two losses were classified as blighted ova. One couple was told that their stillborn baby had died of asphyxiation; the cause given was

TABLE A.1
Type of Death, Classified as Fetal/Infant Death

Type of Death	Number
Fetal Death	
Early fetal death	3
(up to 21 weeks)	
Intermediate fetal death	3
(21 to 28 weeks)	
Late fetal death	3
(over 28 weeks)	
Total fetal deaths	9
Infant Death	
Lived less than 24 hours	6
Lived 1 day to 1 week	4
Lived 1 week to 1 month	4
Lived 1 month to 3 months	2
Lived more than 3 months	2
Total infant deaths	18

TABLE A.2
Type of Death by Time Since Death

Type of Death	Number of Years (N)					
	Under 1	1–2	2–3	3–5	Over 5	Total
Fetal						
Early	2	1	—	—	—	3
Intermediate	—	—	1	1	1	3
Late	—	—	—	1	2	3
Infant						
Lived:						
Under 1 day	—	2	2	1	1	6
1 day to 1 week	—	—	4	—	—	4
1 week to 1 month	1	—	1	2	—	4
1 to 3 months	—	1—	1	—	2	
Over 3 months	—	—	1	—	1	2
Total	4	1	9	9	4	27

TABLE A.3	
Cause of Death (as reported by the parents)	
Type of Death	*Number*
Fetal Death	
Unknown	3
Blighted ovum	2
Asphyxiation	1
Fetal distress	3
toxemia = 1	
high maternal temperature = 1	
premature labor and infection = 1	
Total fetal deaths	9
Infant Death	
Prematurity	6
Genetic defects	3
Congenital abnormalities	7
Spinal meningitis	1
Sudden Infant Death Syndrome	1
Total infant deaths	18

that the umbilical cord had wrapped around his neck. Three fetal deaths were a result of fetal distress: One baby died as a result of the mother's toxemia; one, as a result of the mother's high fever; one was stillborn as the result of the combination of an infection and premature labor. Six infants died as a result of prematurity; their lungs were not sufficiently developed. Other causes given for infant death included probable genetic defects (3) and congenital abnormalities (7), that is, abnormalities that were believed to have originated at some point in the course of intrauterine development. The cause of death for one child was spinal meningitis, and one child died of SIDS.

Recruitment of Participants

Because of the sensitive nature of the topic, it was assumed that the solicitation of a sample would be a complicated, drawn-out process (Gelles, 1978; LaRossa, 1989). In fact, this was the case. Ultimately, participant couples were recruited from a variety of sources: A neo-natal intensive care unit (NICU) of a children's hospital and two sup-port groups in different cities provided the majority of the partici-pants. Other sources were members of the clergy, nurses, mutual acquaintances of the couples and researchers, and other couples who referred themselves upon hearing of the study.

Because of the large number of contact sources and the differing requirements set out by each source, methods of contacting partici-pants differed slightly among groups. As this is the case, the general contact method used will be described here, with additional informa-tion explaining if and how other contact methods differed for a specific group.

Initially, a request was made, by telephone, to a representative of the referring agency or group for couples who had lost a child at any point after 20 weeks' gestation (intermediate and late fetal death) through 1 year after birth (infant death). Couples were to have been married at the time of the death and were to have remained married up until the time of the interview. In addition, the time since death was limited to from 6 months to 5 years. The initial response was small, and because of time and personnel constraints, eligibility was expanded to include early fetal death (before 20 weeks' gestation), and the time since death was expanded to 7 years. These changes were considered legitimate, as it was well under the upper limit of 36 years (Peppers & Knapp, 1980a) and 46 years (Rosenblatt & Burns, 1986) of other qualitative studies of fetal/infant loss.

In most cases, participants were contacted by mail. A brief descrip-tion of the project along with a statement pertaining to the protection of confidentiality, subject rights, anonymity, and so on was included and a response card enclosed on which they could indicate their inter-est in participating in the study. In the case of the first support group, access to the mailing list developed by the representative of the group was not available to the investigator, and interested parents returned a response form that had been sent to them by the representative of the group.

Those who consented to participate were then contacted by tele-phone, and an interview was scheduled at a time and place convenient for them. At this time, arrangements were also made to send the cou-ple a packet containing two copies of a set of the Texas Revised Inventory of Grieving (Faschingbauer, 1981), the Impact of Events Scale (Horowitz, Wilner, & Alvarez, 1979), FACES III (Olson, Portner,

& Lavee, 1985), and informed consent forms for both partners to fill out independently of one another.* Participant couples were then interviewed by two teams of researchers.

The response rate for couples contacted through mail solicitation was low, (20 couples [eight from a support group and 12 from hospital records of the neonatal intensive care unit]). Of these, only 12 participated in the study (five from the support group and seven from hospital records). Parents referred from other sources (including self-referrals) numbered 20. This broke down to three couples from the second support group, five from clergy members, four referred by nurses, five by acquaintances, and three self-referrals. A total of 16 couples from these secondary sources were interviewed.

More women than men expressed an interest in participating, but such individuals were excluded by the criteria of the study. Men consistently have been underreported in bereavement research. Individuals experienced in the area of fetal and infant loss suggested to us that their low participation rate was because of a lack of interest on the part of the men. Other possible explanations for the lower number of men who participate in studies of infant loss include the following: They may fear expressing their emotions, considering this to be "unmanly" and inappropriate; or the wife may be perceived as the family reporter, and the men may, consequently, see the discussion of the loss with others outside the family as an element of that role. Additionally, neither source of participants kept statistics on the current marital status of the parents. Some of the nonparticipants may, therefore, have been divorced or separated at the time they received the letter.

Finally, there was at least some overlap between parents referred by the various sources. Three couples who participated had been contacted through the support group about the study before they were referred by the children's hospital. Other couples, not interested in participating, may have also been referred by both sources.

---

*The original plan of the study was to incorporate both qualitative and quantitative methods. Problems arose with this effort to mix qualitative and quantitative methods. The emergent design (Lincoln & Guba, 1985), which concentrated on the subjective interpretation of the respondents, was ill suited to quantitative methods. Several characteristics of the sample greatly limited the trustworthiness of any quantitative results. These include, but are not limited to: small sample size (27 couples), time since death (6 months to 7 years for the focus loss), range in age of the baby at the time of death (early fetal death through 9 months after birth), the number of other children in the family, and the range of other losses. Because of these problems, the decision was made against using the scales as research instruments but rather as sensitizing agents to "prime" the respondents to think about their loss.

A total of 28 couples were interviewed. Audiotapes of one couple's interview proved to be unintelligible and were not included in this analysis. The sample size (generating 54 interviews) was close to the 20 to 50 range identified by Lofland and Lofland (1984) as the usual for intensive interview studies. They suggested that any larger sample would generate an unmanageable amount of data. Indeed, these interviews resulted in over 1,000 single-spaced, typed pages of data.

DATA COLLECTION

Instruments

DEMOGRAPHIC/HISTORIC INFORMATION

Part A of the interview guide (see Appendix B) was a request for demographic information on themselves—for example, their age, sex, education level, and religious affiliation. Information on the makeup of the family—for example, family size, the ages and sexes of children in the household—was requested. In addition, information on the child who died—for example, sex (if known), age (or approximate gestation) at time of death, cause of death (if known)—was requested.

This information was collected to assess the sample profile and as an aid in determining possible explanations for differences found among the couples in the study. In addition, they were used to compare the participants interviewed by the two research teams.

IN-DEPTH INTERVIEW

Part B of the interview guide consisted of a semistructured, in-depth interview guide (see Appendix C) developed for this study. This served as the primary source of data for this study. It consisted of open-ended questions and probes designed to tap the grief experience of parents as well as the specific aspects of the recovery process. Behavioral as well as subjective aspects of this experience were sought. The form falls between what Patton (1980) has called the general interview guide, a relatively unstructured form, and the standardized open-ended interview. The interview, organized into general topical areas, allowed the participants a frame of reference within which to describe their experience without being constrained to respond to them in one particular fashion (Guba & Lincoln, 1982). In addition, participants were encouraged to follow tangents and present their subjective interpretation of events. It was hoped this type of interview would generate serendipitous information about their experience that had not been anticipated prior to the design of this study.

The interview contained four content areas: The first addressed their experience at the time of and immediately following the death of their child, what needed to be done at that time, what they needed from their spouse, and what they and their spouse did for each other. The second content area concentrated on the ways in which they dealt with their own shadow or recurrent grief and with their spouse's. Third, changes in themselves and their marriage were addressed. Finally, they were asked for recommendations to professionals, family and friends, and other bereaved parents.

The interview guide was evaluated for appropriateness and sensitivity to the parents participating in the study by professionals knowledgeable in the field and by nonparticipant parents who had lost children.

Carrying Out the Interviews

As previously stated, two research teams collected data from couples. With one exception, the interviews took place at the home of the participating couples. In the exception, the couple was interviewed at their family business. Total contact time with the couples ranged from 45 minutes to 4 hours, with taped interviews lasting approximately 50% of that time. The remainder of the time was divided roughly in half between the initial introductions and joining with the couples and the final debriefing at the end of the interviews. The use of co-interviewers allowed both the husband and wife to be interviewed simultaneously. In one case, the husband and wife were interviewed on different dates, because of scheduling problems.

The interview session began with a period of introductions to the interviewers as well as the topic. Participants were encouraged to see themselves as consultants to the project and to ask questions and to offer additional information throughout the interview. The purpose and content of the interview were described to them at this time. In addition, the research teams requested permission to audiotape the interview. Only one person (a husband) refused permission to tape. In that case, careful, extensive notes were taken during the interview and expanded immediately afterwards. In all other cases, participants were informed that, should the tape recorder make them uncomfortable, the interviewer would stop the recorder and notes would be taken. No one chose this option. Both spouses were informed of their option to terminate the interview if they chose. If this option had been exercised, they would have been given all of their materials to do with as they pleased. Again, no one chose to do this.

At this point, the husband and wife moved to separate rooms to be interviewed simultaneously by different interviewers. Both were again informed of their option to terminate the interview if they chose. The interviewer then completed the demographic and historic information (Part A of the interview guide, Appendix B). After this was completed, the interviewer again described the content of the open-ended interview (Part B of the interview guide, Appendix C) and reiterated the option of the participant to terminate the interview. This interview was most evocative of strong emotion and many of the participants, husbands and wives alike, wept. Few held back on their emotions, and they seemed appreciative of an opportunity to express their feelings in a supportive and caring environment.

At the end of the interview, the couple was brought back together for a debriefing period in order for the interviewers to assess their respective emotional states and to avoid leaving them with a feeling that any family secrets had been exposed. At this time, the couple often began to retell the story of their loss, often with the husband and wife taking turns in completing details of the experience. Couples were asked if they wished to receive a copy of the results of the study, and all did. A note, containing telephone numbers of the researchers, was given to the couples in case they wished to contact the researchers or express concerns about the study. In addition, diaries were left behind in case either spouse wished to write any additional information, questions, and concerns that came up during the following week. The purpose of these optional diaries was to make help available to the parents if the interview resulted in problems with recurring memories. Eleven people (five couples and one wife) returned their diaries and of these, two wives included additional information that occurred to them after the interviewer left. No one reported any ill effects from the interviews.

DATA ANALYSIS

Data generated by the interview were analyzed using qualitative means (cf. LaRossa, 1989; Lincoln & Guba, 1985; Patton, 1980). Qualitative analysis includes abstract categorization and discussion of the meaning, application, and implications of the data (Lofland & Lofland, 1984). The data were explored inductively, and the interpretation of the data was idiographic; that is, the emphasis was on particularization rather than generalization (Lincoln & Guba, 1985).

The procedures used in this study followed those suggested by Patton (1980) and LaRossa (1989) and were as follows:

During the data collection phase of the study, field notes were kept of any insights or interpretations that were generated out of the interviews as they occurred. These notes were recorded immediately after leaving the participants' homes as the interview team partners debriefed each other about their immediate impressions. Later, after the tapes had been transcribed, these field notes were included in the more formal data analysis phase.

During the formal data analysis phase, the transcripts were first read once to generate a sense of the total experience for the individual case and across cases. Then, field notes were reread. After this, the interviews were read again, notes were written in the margins of a notation copy, and important passages were underlined. Each case was organized into a case record. At this point, efforts were directed at finding patterns and themes within a particular case (individual or couple) or across cases. Throughout this notation process, notes were kept regarding the types of categories that appeared.

Next, the transcripts were read with the purpose of identifying units within the interviews that could be "pulled" from the transcripts and placed into categories, with provisional rules for inclusion. Later, some of these categories were further broken down while others were combined. As stated above, this was based on thematic patterns within and across cases.

Reliability and Validity

Because of their emergent design and reliance on the human instrument to gather, analyze, and interpret data (Lincoln & Guba, 1985), qualitative methods are subject to questions of reliability and validity. Of particular concern is the threat of bias in reporting (Becker, 1970). These factors cannot be determined for a qualitative study in the same way as they are for a quantitative study—for example, testing reliability statistically for stability over time or for internal consistency. Indeed, the appropriateness of applying these terms to qualitative methods in the same way as they are for quantitative studies has been questioned (Guba, 1978; Kirk & Miller, 1986; Lincoln & Guba, 1985; Patton, 1980). In order to remain consistent with the qualitative paradigm, reliability and validity were assessed using methods suggested by Lincoln and Guba (1985). Plausibility of the account derived from the interviews was assessed by asking others if the results seemed to be a legitimate, unbiased—that is, undistorted and not overly sensitive—description of the bereavement experience. Other researchers involved in this project, nonparticipating bereaved parents, and others knowledgeable in the area of traumatic stress and bereavement were asked if the results seemed to be a legitimate description of the phenomenon. Also, the categories were evaluated with regard to stability across individual cases with particular awareness of the need to find negative cases, or cases that did not fit into the categorization system.

LIMITATIONS

There are several limitations to this study. First, this group is not representative of bereaved parents, and because of this, the findings cannot be generalized beyond other, comparable bereaved parents. This group of individuals has experienced the fetal or infant death of their child. All were married at the time of the child's death and were still married at the time of the interview. Next, all were willing to discuss their child's death in a research setting. The sample included men, a group notoriously underreported in studies of fetal and infant loss (cf. Mandell, et al., 1980; Rosenblatt & Burns, 1968). Finally, the study was restricted to marital pairs.

These and other restrictions mean that caution should be exercised in generalizing from these results. For instance, the characteristics of individuals who lose a child early in life may not be comparable to those of parents who have lost a child at an older age. Different assumptions and expectations may exist for each group. As a result, different issues must be dealt with and different coping methods may be used. Also, the fact that none of the couples were divorced or separated at the time of the interview limits the applicability of the interpersonal dynamics described here to marital couples having similar characteristics.

By requiring that both husband and wife participate, the study was restricted to those couples in which both partners agreed to take part. A number of women who were interested in participating indicated that their husband did not wish to do so. They could not be included. Therefore, it is probable that the men in this study were in some way unique.

It is possible that the individuals who participated in this study had worked through many of the emotions related to their grief and were comfortable in discussing the experience. Several couples also indicated that their participation was motivated by a desire to help other bereaved parents to deal more easily with their grief. The characteristics that led them to be helpers may also be a factor.

Another set of limitations relate to the retrospective nature of this study. Respondents were asked to recall events that had occurred as much as 7 years before. Therefore, there is an element of limited memory that might particularly affect the recall of painful aspects of the experience. In addition, there is also the possibility that participants would have wanted to protect the image of their family and their marriage. In their doing so, misrepresentations and omissions may have taken place. For example, participants showed a tendency to view their spouse in a generally positive light at the time of the interview, reframing behavior they had earlier seen more negatively. This may have been an effort to protect the image of their spouse; it may also have been a way of coping functionally with inconsistency between image and behavior.

Finally, as has been suggested by Rosenblatt and Burns (1986), retrospective studies are not strong in depicting a couple's negotiating process in defining the loss of a child. This limitation, along with the fact that the couples were interviewed separately, prevented a more detailed examination of the negotiation of a shared definition of the loss.

APPENDIX SUMMARY

Twenty-seven couples who experienced the death of their child as a fetus or an infant were recruited from several sources and were interviewed with regard to their bereavement experience following the death of their baby. Marital partners were interviewed separately and simultaneously for information regarding their subjective impressions of the ways in which they both coped with their child's death. This in-depth interview served as the basic source of data for this study. The focus of the data analysis was qualitative and experiential, and explored the subjective meaning of the loss as well as grieving behavior of the respondents.

Appendix B

INTERVIEW GUIDE—PART A
Purdue Bereaved Couple Recovery Research Project

Information in opening statement should be covered before starting the interview schedule: if they have any questions, address them at this time.

PRELIMINARY DATA COLLECTION

(This section consists of collection of demographics and family history taking.)
1. Demographics
    1.1 Sex   M   F
    1.2 Age
    1.3 Occupation
    1.4 When were they married?
    1.5 Member of organized religion? Yes   No
        1.51 If yes, which one?
    1.6 Education level (highest grade/year completed?)
    1.7 Membership in any parent support group? Yes   No
        1.71 If yes, which one(s) and how often does he/she attend meetings?
2. Information on Other Children
    2.1 Any other children in the family? Yes   No
        2.11 If yes, the number of children
        2.12 If yes, the age and sex of each child
    2.2 Have they experienced any other losses? Yes   No
        2.21 If yes, what were these experiences?

2.3 Have they had any other highly upsetting experiences? Yes   No

2.31 If yes, what were these experiences?

3. Information on Deceased Child—(*Note: you may wish to turn the tape recorder on at this point*)

3.1 Able to name the child? Yes   No

3.11 If yes, what is the child's name? (If they were able to name the child, ask for permission to use the child's name during the interview and, if permission is given, REFER TO THE CHILD BY NAME throughout the interview.)

3.2 Position of the child in the birth order (e.g., first child, second child)?

3.3 Child's age at death (if pregnancy, length of pregnancy in weeks)

3.4 How long has it been since death of child?

3.5 Cause of death known? No   Yes

3.51 If yes, what was the cause of death?

3.52 If no, what was the situation at the time? (Probe for why they did not receive an explanation.)

Appendix C

INTERVIEW GUIDE—PART B (husband)*
Purdue Bereaved Couple Recovery Research Project

This portion of the interview schedule is intended to follow part A. If you have not turned on your tape recorder, do so at this time.

Wherever you see (*Wife*) in the interview schedule, insert the name of the interviewee's wife.

PART I—LOSS EXPERIENCE

Reminder: In the choice of terminology, use terms with which the parents are comfortable. Watch for verbal and nonverbal cues.

The purpose of this section is to get a clear picture of his early grief experience and his awareness of his wife's experience. It is important to assess both his emotional and behavioral reactions. Start with the following questions and follow along with him as he recounts his experience.

1. "We would like to know how your child died. Where were you when you found out about your child's death? Where was (Wife)?"

   Probe for whether they were alone or together.

2. "How did you deal with it?"

   Follow his line, if he approaches "you" as singular, follow that line, then ask about how they dealt with it as a couple and vice versa.

   Probe for coping over time, e.g., "What happened after that? What happened after that?"

---

*Wife's interview guide is identical except that the word *husband* replaces the word *wife* and feminine pronouns replace masculine ones.

Probe for how he dealt with it emotionally as well as practically.

PART II—SOCIAL SUPPORT

The purpose of this section is to identify ways in which he and his wife provided support for each other and to identify other sources of support. For clarification, use the following categories of support: Emotional, Informational, and Material.

3. "As you know, this is a time when you need a great deal of support from others. Who helped you and how?" (Note if he mentions his wife without prompting.) "What sort of help did you need from *(Wife)*?"
4. "What sorts of things did *(Wife)* do to help you to get through this time?"
5. "In what way was *(Wife)* not helpful?"
6. "What sorts of things did you do that you felt were helpful?"
7. "What sorts of things did you do that you felt were not helpful?"
8. "What other source of support did you use?"

This does not need to be another person (e.g., books, religion—do not suggest these, let him generate his own list.)

PART III—SHADOW GRIEF

The purpose of this section is to identify their experience with "shadow grief," which consists of reexperiencing of grief, the experience of which may or may not be as intense as their original grief. The image of "a shadow passing over their face" is very helpful in conceptualizing their experience.

9. "Often, as parents begin to recover from their experience of losing a child, many talk about setbacks in their recovery process. Parents talk about reexperiencing intense feelings of loss long after the death of their child. What has your experience of this been?"
10. "What triggers shadow grief for you?"
11. "How did *(Wife)* respond to your reaction to these triggers?"

Probe for helpfulness and lack of helpfulness in dealing with memories.

12. "What sort of experience has (*Wife*) had with shadow grief?"
13. "How have you reacted to her?"

PART IV—CHANGES IN THEMSELVES AND THEIR MARRIAGE

14. "Was there a point at which you decided that you WOULD survive this?"

Probe for a description of his turning point.

15. "How have you changed? What changes do you see in yourself?"
16. "How has your marriage changed? What changes do you see in your marriage?"

PART V—CLOSURE

Transition—"We have talked about your experience of losing a child, how you coped with it as an individual and as a couple. Now I would like to ask you for some help."

17. "Are there any suggestions that you would like to make to people who work with parents who have lost children?" (e.g., medical personnel, therapists, clergy)
18. ". . . to family and friends?"
19. ". . . to other bereaved parents?"

PART VI—DEBRIEFING

• Answer any questions that he has at this time.
• Get both spouses together so that they can discuss anything they would like to talk about together.
• Again, answer any questions they may have.
• Leave a debriefing statement with the phone numbers, addresses of the researchers.
• Leave a diary with the instructions that they are to write in them any questions, comments and/or concerns that come to them during

the next week and return them to principal interviewer (KG or LS) in one week. This is because the interviewing team that went to their home would be more able to answer any questions based on the interview.

• Ask if they would like a copy of the results.

Appendix D

LIST OF PSEUDONYMS

Husband	Wife	Baby
Mason	Nancy	Emma
Roy	Karen	(none)
Henry	Kay	Tina
Peter	Rachel	Andrew
Matt	Jennifer	Amber
Adam	Lynn	Dennis
Stan	Dolores	Donna
Alex	Terry	David
Jonathan	Diane	Maria
Larry	Monica	Pam
Fred	Jane	Jill
Ross	Tamara	Fawn
Roger	Lisa	Sally
Frank	Kelly	Connie
Patrick	Faye	Jeff
Will	Maeve	Jason
Charlie	Willa	Peter
Spencer	Kristina	Timothy
Lance	Melanie	Alan
Ken	Miriam	Brent
Wayne	Gail	Marcie
Ed	Susan	(none)
Phillip	Linda	Buddy
Richard	Cassie	Eric
Nick	Melissa	Scott
Paul	Rose	Micky
Gordon	Rita	Cheryl

Appendix E

LIST OF RESOURCES

When parents experience the loss of a baby, regardless of that baby's age, it may be difficult for them to locate appropriate sources of support and information. The following resource organizations provide support through informational publications and local support groups. Organizations that sponsor local support groups often provide a library for group members. In addition to these groups, local churches and mental health facilities also may sponsor support groups.

Center for Death Education and Research, 114 Social Science Building, University of Minnesota, Minneapolis, MN 55455

Centering Corporation, P.O. Box 3367, Omaha, NE 68103-0367, (402) 553-1200

The Compassionate Friends, Inc., P.O. Box 3696, Oak Brook, IL 60522, (708) 990-0010

Concern for Dying, 250 West 57th Street, New York, NY 10017, (212) 246-6962

The Elizabeth Kübler-Ross Center, South Route 616, Head Waters, VA 24442, (703) 393-3441

The Foundation of Thanatology, 630 West 168th Street, New York, NY 10032

Grief Education Institute, 2422 South Downing Street, Denver, CO 80210, (303) 777-9234

National Center for Death Education, 656 Beacon Street, Boston, MA 02215 ,(617) 536-0194

National Sudden Infant Death Foundation (SIDS), Two Metro Plaza, Suite 205, Landover, MD 20785, (301) 459-3388

Pregnancy and Infant Loss Center, 1415 East Wayzata Boulevard, Suite 22, Wayzata, MN 55391, (612) 473-9372

SHARE, St. John's Hospital, 800 Carpenter, Springfield, IL 62702

SHARE, c/o Sister Jane Marie Lamb, St. Elizabeth's Hospital, 211 South Third Street, Belleville, IL 62222, (618) 234-2120

References

Arnold, J. H., & Gemma, P. G. (1983). *A child dies: A portrait of family grief.* Rockville, MD: Aspen Systems Corp.

Becker, H.S. (1970). Which side are we on? In W. J. Filstead (Ed.), *Qualitative methodology: Firsthand involvement with the social world.* Chicago: Markham Pub. Co.

Benefield, D. G., Lieb, S. A., & Vollman, J. H. (1978). Grief response of parents to neonatal death and parent participation in deciding care. *Pediatrics, 62*(2), 171–177.

Berger, P., & Kellner, H. (1964). Marriage and the construction of reality: An exercise in the microsociology of knowledge. *Diogenes, 46,* 1–25.

Berger, P., & Luckman, T. (1966). *The social construction of reality.* New York: Doubleday.

Blau, Z. S. (1973). *Old age in a changing society.* New York: Franklin Watts.

Blood, R. O., & Wolfe, D. M. (1960). *Husbands and wives: The dynamics of married living.* New York: Free Press.

Bogdan, R. C., & Biklen, S. K. (1982). *Qualitative research in education.* Boston: Allyn & Bacon.

Bogdan, R. C., & Taylor, S. J. (1975). *Introduction to qualitative research methods: A phenomenological approach to the social sciences.* New York: Wiley.

Borg, S., & Lasker, J. (1989). *When pregnancy fails: Families coping with miscarriage, stillbirth and infant death* (rev. ed.). New York: Bantam.

Boss, P. (1987). Family stress. In M. B. Sussman & S. K. Steinmetz (Eds.), *Handbook of marriage and the family* (pp. 695–721). New York: Plenum.

Bowlby, J. (1980). *Attachment and Loss* (Vol. III). New York: Basic Books.

Bugan, L. A. (1983). Childhood bereavement: Preventability and the coping process. In J. E. Schowalter, P. R. Patterson, M. Tallmer, A. H. Kutscher, S. V. Gallo, & D. Peretz (Eds.), *The child and death* (pp. 357–366). New York: Columbia University Press.

Burke, R. J., & Weir, T. (1977). Marital helping relationships: The moderators between stress and well being. *The Journal of Psychology, 95,* 121–130.

Burke, R. J., & Weir, T. (1982). Husband-wife helping relationships as moderators of experienced stress: The "mental hygiene" function in marriage.

In H. I. McCubbin, A. E. Cauble, & J. M. Patterson (Eds.), *Family stress, coping, and social support* (pp. 221–238). Springfield, IL: C. C. Thomas.

Caplan, G. (1974). *Support systems and community mental health*. New York: Behavioral Publications.

Chesler, M. A., & Barbarin, O. A. (1984). Difficulties of providing help in a crisis: Relationships between parents of children with cancer and their friends. *Journal of Social Issues, 40*(4), 113–134.

Chodoff, P., Friedman, S. B., & Hamburg, D. A. (1964). Stress, defenses and coping behaviors: Observations in parents of children with malignant disease. *American Journal of Psychiatry, 120,* 743–749.

Cobb, S. (1982). Social support and health through the life course. In H. I. McCubbin, A. E. Cauble, & J. M. Patterson (Eds.), *Family stress, coping, and social support* (pp. 189–199). Springfield IL: C. C. Thomas.

Cook, J. A. (1988). Dads' double binds: Rethinking fathers' bereavement from a men's studies perspective. *Journal of Contemporary Ethnography, 17,* 285–308.

Cornwell, J., Nurcombe, B., & Stevens, L. (1977). Family response to the loss of a child by Sudden Infant Death Syndrome. *Medical Journal of Australia, 1,* 656–658.

Coyne, J. C., Wortman, C. B., & Lehman, D. R. (1988). The other side of support: Emotional overinvolvement and miscarried helping. In B. H. Gottlieb (Ed.), *Marshalling social support: Formats, processes, and effects* (pp. 305–330). Newbury Park, CA: Sage.

David, D., & Brannon, R. (1976). The male sex role: Our culture's blueprint of manhood and what it's done for us lately. In D. David & R. Brannon, (Eds.), *The forty-nine percent majority: The male sex role* (pp. 1–45). Reading, MA: Addison-Wesley.

Davidson, G. W. (1979). *Understanding the death of the wished-for child*. Springfield, IL: ORG Service Corp.

Dunkel-Schetter, C. (1984). Social support and cancer: Findings based on parent interviews and their implications. *Journal of Social Issues, 40*(4), 77–98.

Eckenrode, J., & Gore, S. (1981). Stressful events and social supports: The significance of context. In B. H. Gottlieb, (Ed.), *Social networks and social support* (pp. 43–68). Beverly Hills, CA: Sage.

Edelstein, L. (1984). *Maternal bereavement: Coping with the unexpected death of a child*. New York: Praeger.

Epstein, N., & Westley, W. (1959). Patterns of intrafamilial communication. *Psychiatric Research Reports, 11,* 1–11.

Farrell, W. (1975). *The liberated man*. New York: Bantam.

Faschingbauer, T. R. (1981). *Texas Revised Inventory of Grief manual*. Houston: Honeycomb Publishers.

Figley, C. R. (1983). Catastrophes: An overview of family reactions. In C. R.

Figley & H. I. McCubbin (Eds.), *Stress and the family. Vol. II: Coping with catastrophe* (pp. 3–20). New York: Brunner/Mazel.

Figley, C. R. (1985). From victim to survivor: Social responsibility in the wake of a catastrophe. In C. R. Figley (Ed.), *Trauma and its wake: The study and treatment of post-traumatic stress disorder* (pp. 398–417). New York: Brunner/Mazel.

Figley, C. R. (1989). Post-traumatic family therapy. In F. Ochberg (Ed.), *Post-traumatic Therapy* (pp. 83–109). New York: Brunner/Mazel.

Filstead, W. J. (1970). Qualitative methods: A needed perspective in evaluation research. In T. D. Cook & C. J. Reichardt (Eds.) *Qualitative and quantitative methods in evaluation research*. Beverly Hills, CA: Sage.

Frantz, T. T. (1984). Helping parents whose child has died. In T. T. Frantz (Ed.), *Death and grief in the family* (pp. 11–26). Rockville, MD: Aspen Systems Corp.

Gelles, R. J. (1978). Methods for studying sensitive family topics. *American Journal of Orthopsychiatry, 48,* 408–424.

Getzel, G. S., & Masters, R. (1984). Serving families who survive homicide victims. *The Journal of Contemporary Social Work, 65*(3), 138–144.

Gilbert, K. R. (1992). Religion as a resource for bereaved parents. *Journal of Religion and Health, 31,* 19-30.

Glaser, B. G., & Strauss, A. L. (1967). *The discovery of grounded theory.* Chicago: Aldine.

Grobstein, R. (1978). The effect of neonatal death on the family. In O. J. Z. Sahler (Ed.), *The child and death* (pp. 92–99). St. Louis: Mosby.

Guba, E. G. (1978). *Toward a methodology of naturalistic inquiry in educational evaluation.* Los Angeles: Center for the Study of Evaluation.

Guba, E. G., & Lincoln, Y. S. (1982). *Effective evaluation.* San Francisco: Jossey-Bass.

Halpern, W. I. (1983). Parental mortification and restitution efforts upon the sudden loss of a child. In J. E. Schowalter, P. R. Patterson. M. Tallmer, A. H. Kutscher, S. V. Gallo, & D. Peretz (Eds.), *The child and death* (pp. 346–354). New York: Columbia University Press.

Hamburg, D. A. (1974). Coping behavior in life-threatening circumstances. *Psychotherapy and Psychosomatics, 23,* 13–25.

Hamburg, D. A., & Adams, J. E. (1967). A perspective on coping behavior. *Archives of General Psychiatry, 17,* 277–284.

Helmrath, T. A., & Steinitz, E. M. (1978). Death of an infant: Parental grieving and the failure of social support. *The Journal of Family Practice, 6,* 785–790.

Hill, R. (1949). *Families under stress.* Westport, CT: Greenwood Press.

Hill, R. (1958). Generic features of families under stress. *Social Casework, 39,* 139–150.

Hoagland, A. C. (1984). Bereavement and personal constructs: Old theories and new concepts. In F. R. Epting, & R. A. Neimeyer (Eds.), *Personal meanings of death: Application of personal construct theory to clinical practice* (pp. 89–109). Washington, DC: Hemisphere.

Hochschild, A., & Machung, A. (1981). *The second shift: Working parents and the revolution at home.* New York: Viking.

Holzner, B. (1968). *Reality construction in society.* Cambridge, MA: Schankman.

Horowitz, M. (1976). *Stress response syndromes.* New York: Jason Aronson.

Horowitz, M. (1979). Psychosocial response to serious life events. In V. Hamilton & D. M. Warburton (Eds.), *Human stress and cognition* (pp. 237–264). New York: Wiley.

Horowitz, M. (1982). Stress response syndromes and their treatment. In L. Goldberger & S. Breznitz (Eds.), *Handbook of stress: Theoretical and clinical aspects* (pp. 711–732). New York: Free Press.

Horowitz, M. (1986). *Stress response syndrome* (2nd ed.) New York: Jason Aronson.

Horowitz, M., Wilner, N., & Alvarez, W. (1979). Impact of Events Scale: A measure of subjective stress. *Psychosomatic Medicine, 41*(3), 209–218.

Janoff-Bulman, R. (1985). The aftermath of victimization: Rebuilding shattered assumptions. In C. R. Figley (Ed.), *Trauma and its wake* (pp. 15–35). New York: Brunner/Mazel.

Janoff-Bulman, R., Madden, M. E., & Timko, C. (1983). Victims' reactions to aid: The role of perceived vulnerability. In J. D. Fisher, A. Nadler, & B. M. DePaula (Eds.), *New directions in helping. Vol. III: Recipient reaction to aid* (pp. 21–29). New York: Academic Press.

Kaplan, D. M., Grobstein, R. & Smith, A. (1976). Predicting the impact of severe illness in families. *Health and Social Work, 1* (3), 72–81.

Kirk, J., & Miller, M. L. (1986). *Reliability and validity in qualitative research.* Beverly Hills, CA: Sage Pub. Co.

Klass, D. (1988). *Parental grief: Solace and resolution.* New York: Springer.

Klauss, M. H., & Kennell, J. H. (1976). *Maternal-infant bonding.* St. Louis: Mosby.

Komarovsky, M. (1973) Cultural contradictions and sex roles: The masculine case. In J. Huber (Ed.), *Changing women in a changing society.* Chicago: University of Chicago Press.

Kübler-Ross, E. (1981). *Living with death and dying.* New York: Macmillan.

Kübler-Ross, E. (1969). *On death and dying.* New York: Macmillan.

LaRossa, R. (1989). In-depth interviewing in family medicine research. In C. Ramsey (Ed.), *Family systems in medicine.* (pp. 227–240). New York: Guilford.

LaRossa, R., & LaRossa, M. M. (1981). *Transition to parenthood: How infants change families.* Beverly Hills, CA: Sage Pub. Co.

Lehman, R. L., Ellard, J. H., & Wortman, B. W. (1986). Social support for the bereaved: Recipients' and providers' perspectives on what is helpful. *Journal of Consulting and Clinical Psychology, 54*(4), 438–446.

Lincoln, Y. S., & Guba, E. G. (1985). *Naturalistic inquiry.* Beverly Hills, CA: Sage.

Lindemann, E. (1944). Symptomatology and management of acute grief. *American Journal of Psychiatry, 101,* 141–148.

Lofland, J., & Lofland, L. H. (1984). *Analyzing social settings: A guide to qualitative observation and analysis* (2nd ed.). Belmont, CA: Wadsworth.

Loftus, E. F. (1979). The malleability of human memory. *American Scientist, 67,* 312–320.

Lopata, H. Z. (1979). *Women as widows: Support systems.* New York: Elsevier.

Mace, D. (1982). *Love and anger in marriage.* Grand Rapids, MI: Zondervan Corp.

Mandell, R. McAnulty, E., & Reece, R. M. (1980). Observations of paternal response to sudden unanticipated infant death. *Pediatrics, 65*(2), 221–225.

Marris, P. (1975). *Loss and change.* London: Routledge & Kegan Paul.

Marris, P. (1982). Attachment and society. In C. M. Parkes & J. Stevenson-Hinde (Eds.), *The place of attachment in human behavior* (pp. 185–204). New York: Basic Books.

McCubbin, H. I., & Patterson, J. M. (1983). The family stress process: The double ABCX model of adjustment and adaptation. *Marriage and Family Review, 6*(1/2), 2–38.

Miles, M. S. (1984). Helping adults mourn the death of a child. In H. Wass & C. A. Corr (Eds.), *Childhood and death* (pp. 219–239). Washington, DC: Hemisphere.

Miller, S. M. (1979). When is a little information a dangerous thing? Coping with stressful events by monitoring versus blunting. In S. Levine & H. Ursin (Eds.) *Coping and health* (pp. 145–170). New York: Plenum.

Morgan, D. (1989). Adjusting to widowhood: Do social networks really make it easier? *The Gerontologist, 29,*(1), 101–104.

Munson, S. W. (1978). Family structure and the family's general adaptation to loss: Helping families deal with the death of a child. In O. J. Z. Sahler (Ed.), *The child and death* (pp. 29–42). St. Louis: Mosby.

Nichols, M. P. (1984). *Family therapy, concepts and methods.* New York: Gardner Press.

Olson, D. H., Portner, J., & Lavee, Y. (1985). *FACES III.* St. Paul, MN: Family Social Science. University of Minnesota.

Osterweis, M., Solomon, F., & Green, M. (1984). *Bereavement: Reactions, consequences and care.* Washington, DC: National Academy Press.

Parkes, C. M. (1972). *Bereavement: Studies of grief in adult life.* New York: International Universities Press.

Parkes, C. M. (1976). Determinants of outcome following bereavement. *Omega, 6,* 303–323.

Patton, M. Q. (1980). *Qualitative evaluation methods.* Beverly Hills, CA: Sage.

Peppers, L. G., & Knapp, R. J. (1980a). Maternal reactions to involuntary fetal/ infant death. *Psychiatry, 43*(Spring), 155–159.

Peppers, L. G., & Knapp, R. J. (1980b). *Motherhood and mourning: Perinatal death.* New York: Praeger.

Rando, T. A. (1980). An investigation of grief and adaptation in parents whose children have died from cancer. Unpublished Ph.D. dissertation, University of Rhode Island.

Rando, T. A. (1983). An investigation of grief and adaptation in parents whose children have died from cancer. *Journal of Pediatric Psychology, 8*(1), 3–20.

Rando, T. A. (1984). *Grief, dying, and death: Clinical interventions for caregivers.* Champaign, IL: Research Press.

Rando, T. (1989, April 20). Anniversary issues and reactions to the death of a child. The eighth annual Kristen Hovda lecture. Evanston Hospital, Evanston, IL.

Raphael, B. (1983). *The anatomy of bereavement.* New York: Basic Books.

Reiss, D. (1981). *The family's construction of reality.* Cambridge, MA: Harvard University Press.

Reiss, D., & Oliveri, M. E. (1980). Family's intrinsic adaptive capacities to its responses to stress. *Family Relations, 29*(4), 431–444.

Rinear, E. (1984). Parental response to child murder: An exploratory study. Unpublished Ph.D. dissertation, Temple University.

Rosenblatt, P. G., & Burns, L. H. (1986). Long-term effects of perinatal loss. *Journal of Family Issues, 7*, 237–253.

Rowe, E. (1982). *The experience of depression.* Chichester, England: Wiley.

Rubin, L. (1976). *Worlds of pain: Life in the working class family.* New York: Basic Books.

Rubin, L. (1983). *Intimate strangers: Men and women together.* New York: Harper & Row.

Ryder, R. G. (1970). Dimensions of early marriage. *Family Process, 9*, 51–68.

Scanzoni, J., & Szinovacz, M. (1980). *Family decisionmaking: A developmental sex role model.* Beverly Hills, CA: Sage.

Schiff, H. S. (1977). *The bereaved parent.* New York: Crown.

Schwartz, H., & Jacobs, J. (1979). *Qualitative sociology: A method to the madness.* New York: Free Press.

Shumaker, S. A., & Brownell, A. (1984). Toward a theory of social support: Closing conceptual gaps. *Journal of Social Issues, 40*, 37–54.

Silver, R. L., & Wortman, C. B. (1980). Coping with undesirable life events. In J. Garber & M. E. P. Seligman (Eds.), *Human helplessness: Theory and applications* (pp. 279–340). New York: Academic.

Smith, J. R. (1981). Veterans and combat: Towards a model of the stress recovery process. Paper presented for the Veterans Administration Operation Outreach Training Program, 1980.

Stephenson, J. S. (1985). *Death, grief and mourning: Individual and social realities.* New York: Free Press.

Symonds, M. (1980). The "second injury" to victims. *Evaluation and Change,* 36–38.

Taylor, S. E. (1983). Adjustment to threatening events: A theory of cognitive adaptation. *American Psychologist, 38,* 1161–1173.

Taylor, S. E., Lichtman, R. R., & Wood, J. V. (1987). Attribution, beliefs about control and adjustment to breast cancer. *Journal of Personality and Social Psychology,*

Thompson, L., & Walker, A. J. (1982). The dyad as the unit of analysis: Conceptual and methodological issues. *Journal of Marriage and the Family, 44,* 901–926.

Walker, A. (1985). Reconceptualizing family stress. *Journal of Marriage and the Family, 47,* 827–836.

Waller, W. (1967). *Old loves and the new: Divorce & readjustment.* Carbondale, IL: Southern Illinois Press.

Watzlawick, D., Weakland, J., & Fisch, R. (1974). *Change: Principles of problem formation and problem resolution.* New York: Norton.

Weitzman, S. G., & Kamm, P. (1985). *About mourning: Support and guidance for the bereaved.* New York: Human Sciences Press.

Wortman, C. B., & Dunkel-Schetter, C. (1979). Interpersonal relationships and cancer: A theoretical analysis. *Journal of Social Issues, 35*(1), 120–155.

Wortman, C. B., & Silver, R. C. (1989). The myths of coping with loss. *Journal of Consulting and Clinical Psychology, 57*(3), 349–357.

Name Index

Subject Index